Presented To:

TAT AKA MUM
AKA GRANDMA AKA SISTER

From:

Kim + Lil Peep

Date:

14-3-21
mothers day

Surviving Domestic Violence

A SIMPLE GUIDE TO BREAKING FREE

Books That Enrich You
To Enrich Others

Books that bless the heart and soothe the soul. Whether you are seeking to invest a little something into your personal development, or whether you simply need a shot of inspiration to fuel your aspirations.

Open Scroll Publications offers a new breed of books designed to impact the mind, touch the heart, and ignite the spirit.

SURVIVING DOMESTIC VIOLENCE

A SIMPLE GUIDE TO BREAKING FREE

DIANE WILKIE

Published by Open Scroll Publications

Copyright © 2019 by Diane Wilkie

Email: dee.wilkie7@hotmail.co.uk
Visit: survivedomesticviolence.simplesite.com

First published 2019 by:
Open Scroll Publications Ltd,
Kemp House, 160 City Road,
London, EC1V 2NX.
www.openscroll.co.uk

ISBN 978-1-9999856-0-8

Cover design and Typeset by Open Scroll Publications.

All abbreviations are taken from the Concise English Dictionary
Omega books Ltd copyright © Cassell Ltd. 1962
New material © Cassell Ltd. 1964, 1966,1968

Scripture quotations are taken from the Holy Bible, New Living Translation, copyright © 1996. Used by permission of Tyndale House Publishers, Inc, Wheaton, Illinois 60189. All rights reserved.

Printed in Great Britain.

DEDICATION

This book is dedicated to every person who has ever been threatened, felt afraid, or been hurt directly or indirectly by the crime of domestic violence.

It is dedicated also to every one of those precious people who have sadly lost their lives, directly because of this hideous plague of society. It is also dedicated to their family members who have been left behind and forced to cope with the excruciating pain of their loss.

ACKNOWLEDGMENTS

This book is written in honour of every woman and child that I was blessed enough to meet at the refuge, where I worked for eleven years. Every single one of you displayed an admirable ability and fierce determination to overcome the harsh reality of surviving and being affected by domestic violence. I salute you!

I have huge respect also for all those people everywhere, (including all the men who have been bullied, and suffered greatly), what can only be described as a violation of your free will. You are all such an inspiration and incredibly brave! Thank you for your willingness to share your own unique story. You never know, you may just have given someone else the courage to come forward also, to tell others what they have been going through. Who knows, maybe that was just the push they needed, to put a stop to the suffering they have been experiencing in silence!

I would also like to say a huge thank you to all the different agencies out there, who make so much of a difference to all the vulnerable women and children who come to you. No doubt so many times your job may have been a thankless one! The lives of these precious people however have been helped immeasurably and made better and richer because of you! You have done something far more than words can ever express….You have made a difference!

I want to thank my husband Nigel, for teaching me that loving someone is one of life's most precious gifts, and that it should not hurt, break your heart and wound your soul!

Finally, a huge thank you to my publisher Open Scroll Publications — you are a God-send!

CONTENTS

WARNING!!! SOME OF THE REAL-LIFE STORIES IN THIS BOOK ARE QUITE GRAPHIC. PLEASE BE AWARE THAT SOME READERS MAY FIND THEM DISTRESSING.

Many of the names and identifying details of some individuals mentioned in this book have changed, to protect their privacy.

AN OPENING THOUGHT

WHY WRITE A BOOK ABOUT DOMESTIC VIOLENCE?

According to statistics at least one in every three women will most likely have been beaten, coerced and pressured into having sex, or abused in some other way including being raped, at some point in their lives! This is absolutely astounding and adds up to a phenomenal number of women! This is a horrendous world-wide, problem that doesn't seem to be going away any time fast! Although it is slowly being addressed to a certain extent, it is still a major big deal because it has reached unacceptable and critical proportions! It is still way too common and happening too often in many households, often behind closed doors. There is therefore vast room for improvement in every sense. Society at large must raise awareness and become mindful that it goes on, even in the twenty first century!

Domestic violence has continued to be a growing force that has become stronger until unfortunately it has become an epic disaster. This cannot be taken lightly. Neither should it be thought of as 'just one of those things, that is accepted by society! No matter what part of the world it is, it will never be right or acceptable! It is criminal and should be treated as such!

Many people unfortunately 'feel clueless,' when it comes to knowing how best to help someone who is suffering from domestic violence. They are often plagued with questions about the best way to handle things, how to support the victim, and indeed what to say to them!

Many years ago, when I was in my early thirties, I became

involved in an abusive relationship. It was with a young man that I will call Robert. When we first met I was quite taken with how tall, dark, moody and mysterious he was. Once the novelty wore off however and reality hit, I suddenly found myself on the floor with him literally physically restraining me, holding me down on the ground so that I couldn't move away from him, even though I desperately wanted to. He was of a big build, and at 6ft 4inches tall he was so much bigger and stronger than me. There was nothing I could do but stay there until he decided to release me. He held me there against my will for what felt like an eternity! I felt totally humiliated, frustrated and helpless. I was so ashamed for allowing him to do this to me, so much so that I didn't tell a single soul about the incident for years until much later.

He always made me feel as if I was privileged to be breathing in the same air as him, never mind be with him! He mentally and emotionally abused me whenever he felt like it, and shockingly I remained in this relationship for two years! I did not realize that I was worth more than that, or that I deserved any better than he was offering! I always thought that one day if I did not give up on him, and just loved him enough, that he would change. I was incredibly naïve back then! No matter how much I tried to love him, he kept moving the goal posts and it was never enough, or acceptable to him. He seemed to get a kick out of treating me as if I was just something he found on the bottom of his shoe!

Before we met he had been engaged to be married to someone else. At the last minute she changed her mind and let him down. He took it badly. When we met shortly afterwards therefore, our relationship was doomed, hopeless and destined to fail. He hadn't recovered and was not equipped to be in another relationship. I on the other hand was under some illusion that I could fix him. The only problem was that it felt like his mission in life had become, to get revenge for all he had been through, and make me pay for everything she had done to him! There was only one thing I managed to succeed in doing, and that was enabling him to be abusive towards me!

Inevitably our relationship imploded and thankfully disintegrated and we parted company, before I wasted any more time on him and completely ruined my whole life! The whole experience tore me up inside and ripped my self-confidence to shreds. I was devastated by the utter failure of the relationship and my inability to fix his kind of 'sickness.' The main thing I came away with was a desperately wounded soul. I was however still alive and determined to pick myself up off the ground and start again. I refused to end up as just another 'statistic!' Instinctively I knew there was more to life than this, and most definitely life after the abuse of domestic violence! I just needed to be re-educated regarding what a healthy relationship looked like, and I needed to learn fast.

Sometimes when people fall off a horse, they either go lick their wounds, or they get straight back on the horse, more determined than ever to never fall off again. I certainly shocked myself and proved to be the latter. The whole experience turned out to be a blessing in disguise. I learned what an unhealthy relationship looked like and how much I didn't want one!

After a few false starts, the right man eventually turned

up and found me! (It was such a refreshing change to not have to go looking for Mr Right)! I know he is the right man because one of the greatest gifts he has given me, is the encouragement and freedom to just be myself. He loves and accepts me for who I am, but still nurtures me in the areas where I do need to change and grow as a person.

On the 24th of August (this year 2019), we would have been married for seventeen amazing years! Our marriage has not always been plain sailing or a walk in the park. However, any married couple will tell you that marriage takes commitment, hard work, and a generous dose of unconditional love and forgiveness simultaneously.

The point is however, that our relationship is essentially healthy at its core, and therefore stands a chance. That means that the love and respect necessary to make it work are present. All parties remain safe and can enjoy the blessing of having that special 'someone to love.' There is no fear present of serious repercussions, or damage to anyone's health! Having experienced relationships from both angles, it is no longer rocket science to me which type is preferable!

This is the reason for this book. I want to say something to every person, (man, woman, or child) going through the hell of domestic violence right now, "**YOU CAN BREAK FREE!**" Domestic violence is most definitely a life shattering experience however, it does not have to be the thing that defines you, or signals the end of your life, or story!

Other people who have previously been victims, have not had to die without hope in their seemingly impossible situations! Many have not only survived but have used their experience, as launch pads for bigger, better and greater things in life! The great news is that "YOU CAN TOO!" After all, why should you be the one to settle for less than life has to offer? If there is any difference between you and them, it would only be a question of mindset. Theirs told them they could, while perhaps yours is telling you that you cannot!

The fact that others have successfully done it, proves that with strength of mind, anything is possible if you want it badly enough! It is important that you give a voice to the victims of this crime. You can get over the devastation and crushing impact. You do this by talking about it. You must get real, so that you can deal with and end its devastating effect on you.

After my unfortunate experience with an abuser, I got a job in a refuge, working closely with women and children, supporting them as victims of domestic violence. I didn't go looking for this type of job, but somehow it seemed right that this had become my vocation. Subsequently this was my job for eleven years, until circumstances changed, and I felt it was time to move on. Part of moving on, meant writing this book. I wanted to share what I had learned, with those who have only just begun their journey out of domestic violence, but perhaps don't feel they have a map.

It has been a very challenging but rewarding career, one that has been a real honour. I consider it to have been a real blessing to have had such an amazing opportunity. The thing I enjoyed the most about the job was supporting every courageous woman, that walked through the refuge door. Being present to be able to witness their progress, along an almost impossible journey, and knowing that some-how I made a difference to them, when they were at their most vulnerable, is an indescribable privilege! The many women and children I have worked with over the years have proven that indeed, heroes of this life are not always the obvious ones. In fact often they are the unlikely ones hidden in obscurity. It is to these courageous people that this book is dedicated to. Working with you has taught me so much! I am so proud of all that you have overcome, and I take my hat off to you all!

Proverbs 31: 8-9 NEW LIVING TRANSLATION says, **"Speak up for those who cannot speak up for themselves, ensure justice for those being crushed. Yes, speak up for the poor and helpless, and see that they get justice**."

This is the point of this book; that the voiceless will find and have a voice that is loud, strong, free and beautiful in its expression! Let's not keep destiny waiting any longer, but together let's break off the chains that have held us captive and shatter the silence with an ear piercing, shout of freedom, knowing that FREEDOM IS WORTH THE FIGHT!

Diane Wilkie

1

What Is Domestic Violence?

Aggressor: One who begins a quarrel. To attack, assault.

Violence: Violent exercise of power. An act of intimidation by the show or threat of force. Violent treatment, injury.

Abuse: To put to improper use, violation, misuse

(The Concise English Dictionary)

A person who treats another person or animal with cruelty or violence, especially regularly or repeatedly.

(The Oxford Dictionary)

D omestic violence takes place whenever a person uses abusive and manipulative behaviour, to control another person. Often this occurs within a relationship type scenario, where a person literally abuses their power over the other person. Essentially it amounts to the victim being bullied by the person being aggressive towards them. This behaviour, can and often is accompanied by violence, (even the threat of it is enough, to stop the victim in their tracks)! The aim is to intimidate the victim and force them to comply, doing whatever the abuser decides has got to happen! The victim is left feeling as if they must give up even their basic human right, of having the power to choose!

Many times, domestic violence is suffered by women at the hands of men. It is however important to establish, that it obviously is not always the case. Sometimes, it is in fact the other way around. We do however have to face the fact, that a lot of the time, violence against women is indeed the unfortunate reality.

Often it is a complete mystery ... WHY ON EARTH DO WOMEN STAY IN ABUSIVE RELATIONSHIPS? Why don't they just get up and leave? On the surface these are simple enough questions. However the answers are much more complicated.

Often, they stay with an abusive partner generally, due to incorrect thinking. They become trapped by the false notion, that the domestic violence they suffer from is somehow their fault. They come to believe that if they had not done or said certain things, they would not have provoked him! They have often been told they deserve to be abused anyway. Before long, lies and reality become entwined to such an extent, that soon it is impossible for them to make a clear distinction between the two.

Mistakenly they often believe their love is strong enough to change their partner. It is as if they have temporarily forgotten, that this same person continues to choose to be aggressive towards them. Things get hazy and they don't always manage to see that this is wrong and will never be right under any circumstances!

Sometimes it is as simple as them thinking they won't be believed, if they told anybody. At other times they are so gripped by fear, that their abuser will harm and even kill them if they tell anyone. It is so easy for them to come to believe that, they are the only one in the world that this could possibly be happening to!

Although the victim often spends majority of their time crippled by fear in the relationship, for them in many ways the 'fear' of the unknown is so much worse. The violence has become so normal to them, that they cannot even comprehend leaving the situation. They are just too afraid to take the necessary steps to change things, because of all the uncertainty that change would inevitably bring.

A good example of this is when they have become financially dependent. When they have no money of their own, and have always depended financially on the abuser, it is not so easy for the victim to separate themselves from the relationship and go somewhere else. Sometimes it is the sheer fear of the expense of starting all over, that forces them to stay put. They would have to get a new home, and basically start a whole new life! It is perhaps not easy to even comprehend, the possibility of having their own money, or the knowledge of managing their own money, especially when they have never had to do it before. The truth is, it is not easy to leave! If it was, victims would just get up and leave every single day.

It was also my experience in talking to the women at the refuge, that sometimes a woman would stay in a violent relationship for the sake of her children. If they ever did get the courage to leave they were often riddled with guilt. They felt bad about uprooting and removing the children from the family home. Over time they had become so worn down, that they felt as if they were the one breaking up the family and taking the kids away from their father. Unfortunately for some, the guilt of this was just too much. It was made more difficult, especially when the kids tearfully continued to ask to see their dad!

Staying in a violent relationship, can be down to a victim feeling paralyzed by pressure from family members. This could be their own family or the abuser's family. A good example of this is in the Asian culture where families (including in-laws), often all live together in one house. In this kind of scenario, the woman often feels as if she not only married her husband, but in fact married his whole family. Victims can therefore experience violent assault from their husband, as well as from family members. I know of women who literally lived as slaves in the home. When they got married, unfortunately they literally got much more than they bargained for.

Domestic violence never seems to discriminate. It can in fact be seen and experienced across the board. Apparently, it affects every background, culture, age group, religion, race as well as the educated and uneducated.

When I first started to work at the refuge, a few things really shocked me. In the first instance, I could not believe how common it was! Before that I did not realize it was indeed an everyday occurrence, and that so many people experienced it! The refuge I worked at was a very big one, and yet it was always full and operating at maximum capacity! In fact sometimes sadly we even had no choice but to turn women away, after signposting them to where else they could get alternative help.

There are countless situations in which domestic violence can and often does take place. It can be found within intimate relationships between husbands and wives, (where either can be the abuser), boyfriends and girlfriends, siblings, parents and children. There does not seem to be any hard and fast rules about when or why it happens. When it does take place, it has long lasting effects, usually successfully devastating the lives of the victims involved.

2

Signs And Symptoms Of Domestic Violence

PART ONE: THE FEAR FACTOR

Some very crucial questions to ask yourself include:

- Do you ever literally feel afraid for your very life?

- Do you think to yourself, that if he ever got hold of you physically one last time — he would kill you for sure?

- Have you ever heard of anyone or know someone that has died because of domestic violence?

- Does this frighten you and make you think seriously about your own circumstances?

- Does he ever become abusive to the kids as well?

- Do you put yourself in the middle (between him and them), taking a beating just to try and protect your children?

- Have you ever decided to leave him because you became so worried and scared for your children?

- Have you ever decided to go to the police and press charges one minute, and then at the crucial moment drop them all the next?

- Does he drive too fast when you are in the car, to scare you into whatever he demands of you?

- Does he use bullying tactics, banging, smashing and breaking things to make you jump, and keep you feeling like a nervous wreck all the time?

- Does he use an intimidating tone of voice when he speaks to you, so that you are living in a never ending, bubble of heightened fear?

- Does he invade your personal space, getting right up in your face showing the ultimate disrespect for you as a person….as a fellow human being?

- Does he make loud noises and sudden movements so that it is literally impossible for you to relax?

- Does he forbid you to express an opinion of your own or break one of the rules he has set and commanded you to obey?

- Does he constantly move the goal posts, so you feel as if you can't do right for doing wrong, and just have to keep jumping through numerous hoops, all the time?

- Does he regularly kick the doors and break the windows of your family home for maximum effect?

- Does he physically restrain you so that you cannot choose to move away from him, no matter how much you want to?

- Does he lock you in the house, so that you are a prisoner in your own home?

- When he does allow you to go out, does he time you and then punish you for breaking his curfew?

- Does he intimidate members of your family and your friends so that they are so uncomfortable when they come to visit, that they don't come back, until you are completely isolated?

- Does he carry out his plan to destroy your support network, so that you are completely dependent on him because you have no-one else?

- If he has raped you, have you been too afraid to report the crime to the police?

Fear is a major tactic used by the abuser to establish exactly who is boss. He uses control and manipulation simultaneously to go to work on his victim. Ultimately, his aim is to ensure that eventually his victim is systematically worn down over time. This could be over a short period of time like a sprint race, or over a longer time frame like a marathon instead.

As the victim is worked on, someone who was once so confident, full of life and all its promise, becomes notably dull, lifeless, jumpy, full of fear, with little or no sense of self-worth or esteem. Fear of not wanting to upset the apple cart and the abuser, becomes their new motivation and drive in life. It is unfortunately a lost cause. The abuser is never satisfied and hardly ever impressed, because he becomes the expert at the art of continually moving the goal posts. Soon the victim is jumping through every hoop imaginable. This however is all to no avail because she can never truly know exactly what he actually expects from her! This is mostly because he doesn't even know for sure himself but makes it up as he goes along!

Often at first (when the relationship is new fresh), it is typical for the abuser to pursue his victim relentlessly refusing to take no for an answer, (all in the name of love of course). Soon however the promises he made start to get broken, and he is no longer Mr nice guy (the one you fell in love with)!

Before long you start to see disturbing signs as he becomes pushy, and continuously ignores and forces his way past the boundaries you try to set.

His controlling behaviour, cannot hide forever and his true colours are revealed soon enough. As a result, the man who could not do enough for you, becomes the man who refuses to lift a finger to help you, even when the children come along!

Sure enough, he starts to push you around in front of the them, and the fact that you may be holding one of them in your arms at the time, makes no difference to him at all! Anything and everything sets him off, and nothing you do pleases him.

He gets upset when the children cry and accuses you of loving even a helpless little baby more than you love him. Surely this is the height of pathetically sick behaviour! The crux of the matter boils down ultimately to being all about control! He just loves and gets a kick out of seeing fear in your eyes!

- Have you ever had to leave the property where you live because you are afraid of him and what he might do to you?

- Did you then have to return to the property when he was out, to collect your belongings, clothes, valuables, kids toys?

- Did you feel as if your heart was in your mouth, as you wondered whether he would return unexpectedly before you had a chance to escape?

- Does he manage to find you even when you move out of the area?

- Has he ever used the children to find out the information about where you have moved to?

- Does he mess with your head by saying things like, "I will never allow you to take away my kids," or "you know you can't live without me!"

- Do you spend most of your life on the run, ducking and diving?

- Has it become necessary to spend the other half of your life looking over your shoulder, wondering if he or someone he knows, will see you and start the whole violent cycle again?

- Do you ache and long for your life to start all over again without this unwelcome added complication?

It is important for you to know and accept that he will often stop at nothing to break you down. As far as he is concerned, you are his woman and therefore belong to him. The questions in his mind are and always will be, "how dare you even consider having a life without his say so, or worse without him?"

- Does he threaten to kill you if you ever leave him?

- Does he shout you down, and intimidate you if and whenever you try to stand up to him?

PART TWO

FORMS OF ABUSE

SECTION ONE

PHYSICAL ABUSE

Often the abuse suffered is of a violent physical nature.

- Do you ever tell yourself in desperation that, 'he won't hurt me again, even though you know in your heart that you stare death full in the face more often than you would like to admit?'

- Do you try and convince yourself that this is the last time he will ever physically hurt you?

- Have you ever been hit, shaken, burned with a cigarette or otherwise?

- Have you been pinched, suffocated, kicked, punched, slapped, pushed, bitten, even poisoned?

- Has your partner ever tried to drown you?

- Has he driven a car recklessly until you were afraid you were going to die there and then?

- Has your partner smashed up your belongings in an attempt to forcibly control you?

- Have you been physically held against your will at any time?

- Have you had things thrown at you?

- Have you ever ended up bruised and bleeding, because of being violently assaulted?

- Have you ever ended up with black eyes or broken bones?

- Have you ever ended up in hospital as a result of him physically assaulting you?

- Do you flinch when he raises his hand or voice, or even when he walks towards or comes near you?

It does not matter if it happened only once or again and again. There is usually an absolute uproar when animals are treated cruelly. How much more should there be when one human being believes they have the right to injure, harm, violate and even kill another human being. Their reasoning… they do it just because they can, and because they feel they are not accountable to any-one! There will never be an excuse valid enough to justify this barbaric behaviour. Please come to terms with this truthful fact! THIS IS NOT NORMAL HEALTHY BEHAVIOUR!

If any of the above is happening to you or to someone you know, please speak up and get some help for yourself. (See page 123 with helpful contact details) You should know there are options available to you, as this is the twenty first century! The number one person who has the power to change your situation is you. If you choose to do nothing about it, then you will simply waste years of your life, going around and around in circles or worse!

A major key and step in the right direction, is recognizing that the treatment that you are being subjected to and receiving is inappropriate, unhealthy, unacceptable and a crime against your human rights. Your role in fighting against the perception therefore, that one human being has a right to ruthlessly dominate another, is an absolute crucial factor when it comes to gaining your freedom! More on this in later chapters! The good news to hold on to, is that this does not need to continue to be a hopeless situation. You can become equipped to make different choices!

In 2012 Melissa Dohme a twenty one year old lady, was subjected to a case of extreme domestic violence where she was attacked by her ex-boyfriend. They had broken up three months prior to the attack, however he refused to accept that the relationship was over.

On the 21st of January 2012 he made his move, revealing his unmistakable aim. He planned to kill her, stabbing her thirty-two times in total. She suffered from stab wounds to her head, neck, face, hands and arm as she tried in vain to protect herself. She haemorrhaged severely from arteries that had been cut in her neck. She died four times and had to be resuscitated, suffered a stroke and a fractured skull, a broken nose, and lost some teeth. She needed twelve units of blood as she had lost so much of her own.

Shockingly, although she had every reason to, she refused to go into victim mode! She came to an astonishing conclusion. It was her firm belief that God saved her life for a unique purpose. That purpose is to tell others about what happened. By sharing her story, she felt compelled to become a voice. A voice for all those who are too afraid to speak. Presently she works tirelessly as their advocate. She is a perfect example of the incredible truth.... DOMESTIC VIOLENCE DOES NOT HAVE TO BE THE THING THAT DEFINES YOU! Nor does it have to be the end of your particular story!

Similarly, a twenty year old pregnant woman, got involved with a man she didn't know very much about. She had no idea unfortunately, that he had a criminal past, as well as a dark history of violent assault, against two previous girlfriends.

As things did not seem quite right, one day she decided that the relationship was no longer for her, so she expressed this to him. Without hesitation he seemed to go absolutely crazy, reacting to the news by punching her in the stomach. As a result, the very next day she started to miscarry their unborn child. When she got to the hospital a scan revealed that the baby she was carrying had died. What happened although unacceptable, unfortunately is the kind of thing that happens more commonly, than is comfortable to acknowledge!

Another young lady Malorie Bantala who was thirty two weeks pregnant, was brutally attacked by her ex-boyfriend and an accomplice in the street. They pushed her to the ground and then cowardly killed her unborn child by stamping on her stomach repeatedly. Eventually, once they had inflicted as much damage as possible they ran off, leaving her for dead. She received emergency first aid treatment, but unfortunately, they could not save the baby, and she herself ended up in intensive care with life threatening internal bleeding. Eventually the attackers were caught and sent to prison. To add salt to the wound, Malorie found out also, that after her ordeal there is a chance that she may not be able to have any children. Presently Malorie campaigns for a change in the child destruction law, to be extended to covering unborn babies also.

On March 2016, (on the news) just outside a church, a forty one year old man violently and brutally attacked a 40 year old heavily pregnant woman in the street. At the time it was down to two good Samaritans who were passing, to intervene and assist this helpless bleeding woman. During the incident they put themselves at risk, for the sake of this lady and ended up with minor injuries themselves. The woman was later air lifted by air ambulance to the hospital. She gave birth to a baby who was reported to be doing well. The mother on the other hand was said to be critical. Two days after the incident the abuser was arrested and charged with two counts of attempted murder. This was referred to as 'a domestic related situation,' by the police.

For some reason pregnancy is often a catalyst for domestic violence. In fact, it has been known to at times be the thing that actually sets it off. In other cases, although it may always have been present, it can certainly escalate to new levels during pregnancy. The abuse of power thrives at the very sight of vulnerability. The demand that the abuser puts on the relationship to always be the center of attention, obviously goes out the window once a pregnancy takes place. These are some of the reasons for such developments.

Another lady was stabbed in the face and then had Sulphuric acid poured over her. The abuser's intention, and plan was basically to disfigure his ex. After this horrendous attack, she ended up losing an ear, becoming partially bald, and permanently disfigured. Before this attack, there was another incident where he had locked her in his flat for hours, threatening her throughout the whole ordeal. It was his usual habit to rape her whenever he felt like it!

It was actually because of his behaviour, that she finally found the courage to leave the relationship. The acid attack was the result. His sick reasoning was that if he could not have her, then he would make sure no other man could, or even would want her!

Looking at things from a different perspective now, there is another aspect of physical abuse that is also difficult to understand. This occurs when a man is suffering from domestic violence at the hands of his female partner. As it is a presumed fact that men are generally physically stronger than women, it is incredibly difficult to fathom how this could be possible. Men who experience this, may even be ridiculed as a result. Many men feel intense shame because of the stigma attached, and so they probably would find it so difficult to tell anyone, never mind come forward. For a man the difficulty is increased, because of the stereotyping involved. Men suffering from domestic violence is more difficult to accept, because of course it is punctuated by the question.... 'how could a man who is obviously stronger than a woman, allow her to bully and actually injure him?'

Men who suffer from domestic violence are particularly challenged, because there are not many refuges that are geared towards them, or appropriate for them to go to. There is quite a lack of funding for such services, and hardly any leaflets with information that would help them. The media hardly ever highlight such cases. Occasionally however there are exceptions.

On the 13th of March 2015, Ken Gregory, a male victim of domestic violence came forward to the media to share his story. He was even brave enough to show the horrendous scars on his body. The reason he did this was to encourage other men who are suffering from the same kind of physical abuse, to feel that they can also come forward.

His own unique story came to light when he was attacked by his ex-wife, who thought it was perfectly acceptable to pour a kettle of hot boiling water over his head badly scarring his back! On another occasion as he lay asleep in bed, she poured a hot cup of tea on him. She was very creative, when it came to thinking of new ways of abusing him.

Domestic violence can happen at any time at all. The prejudice that the victim can feel, whether they are male or female, can and often does affect their decision regarding whether to come forward or not.

Working at the refuge I saw things which unfortunately will stay with me, for as long as I live. I have haunting memories of having to receive many women directly from the casualty of a hospital. This was usually necessary to receive treatment for the physical injuries they had received, at the hands of their partners. It was a common and regular thing. It did not matter how long I worked there, the sight of injured, vulnerable, broken women always got to me. I would however force myself to focus on doing my job. It was up to me to provide practical and emotional help and support. That I tried to do to the very best of my ability in spite of the challenges of the job.

Another story of incredibly bravery. A lady was sitting in the driver's seat of her car with her boyfriend in the passenger seat. He aggressively commanded her to hand over her phone. When she refused to do so, he punched her in the face. He then proceeded to choke her, in a determined effort to wrestle her phone away from her by extreme force, till she started bleeding! After what seemed like forever, eventually, he allowed her to drop him off to where he lived. She was so relieved to be able to then continue her journey home alone. At the time it seemed as if he had won, as he was obviously physically stronger than she was. He had masterfully succeeded at exerting his will and violating hers at the same time.

This was not treatment she suffered at the hands of a stranger by the way. Rather this was a trusted man whom she had known as a friend for many years. They had started dating a few months prior to this incident occurring.

I greatly commend this lady and take my hat off to her. Considering the seriousness of what happened to her, she could very well have curled up into a little ball never to have been heard from again. Instead however, in spite of the trauma she suffered, she decided to allow her friend (who just happened to be a photographer), to take photos of her, displaying in graphic detail the injuries she suffered. The idea was to expose the crime of domestic violence, while raising awareness about this incredibly uncomfortable subject. She felt the need to become the face and real-life example, of someone changed forever by the horror of domestic violence. It was no longer good enough, for it just to come down to one more statistic. No, it was her most sincere hope that others would find the courage to follow suit, come forward, and tell their equally disgusting story.

The photographer friend posted these photos on her Facebook photography business website, and the effect was astronomical! People everywhere began to comment, and send messages, all eager to reach out and connect. It literally went viral and no-one was as shocked or surprised as the two women involved. They never envisaged or imagined on any level, that what they had done would have such an incredible response and effect. 'Silence hides Violence,' therefore was the result and the campaign that was subsequently launched.

Domestic violence does not discriminate. To emphasize this point, notably we can look at a few of the high profile, well publicized cases here of the celebrities who have been victims at some time or another.

Tina Turner had major issues with her husband Ike. She suffered tremendous physical and mental abuse from him. He took drugs and was constantly unfaithful to her. His behaviour towards her was so controlling, that when he apparently 'discovered,' her as an artist, he changed her name from Anna Mae Bullock to Tina Turner, as she famously came to be known. He was known to violently attack her until she bled. He even broke her jaw once. There did finally come a time when she decided enough was enough and she wanted out! She escaped for the final time one night as he lay sleeping. She had no choicc but to clean houses to earn money to pay her rent during those days. She soon however found the courage to go solo as an artist and began to make song hits. The rest is history.

Similarly, Boy George, (George Alan O'Dowd) shared his story during an interview, about how domestic violence plagued his childhood. He admitted to having a complicated relationship with his dad, especially as it was characterized by physically violent, disturbing, outbursts. His dad had a bad temper, which often erupted and would end up with the over-turning of the Sunday dinner, and the whole family going hungry that day. This no doubt affected him greatly.

ENDNOTES

1. https://www.christianpost.com/news/god-saved-me-woman-forgives-ex-boyfriend-who-stabbed-her-32-times.html By Morgan Lee, Christian Post Reporter n.d

2. https://www.dailymail.co.uk/news/article-3364457/Thug-stamped-pregnant-girlfriend-killing-baby-refused-abortion-GUILTY-accomplice-savage-attack.html By Amanda Williams for mail online 17th of December 2015

3. https://www.theguardian.com/uk-news/2015/aug/17/man-in-court-alleged-stabbing-acid-attack-ex-girlfriend Monday 17th of August 2015

4. https://www.mirror.co.uk/news/uk-news/pensioner-horrifically-scarred-after-wife-5324460 By Ben Kendall 13th of March 2015

5. https://www.sofeminine.co.uk/key-debates/silence-hides-violence-campaign-against-domestic-abuse-s1555443.html By Maria Bell 8th of September 2015

6. https://people.com/music/tina-turner-ike-abusive-relationship-risked-life/ By Jorden Runtagh October 26th 2017

7. https://metro.co.uk/2017/02/17/viewers-praise-boy-george-for-brave-comments-about-domestic-abuse-in-his-family-6456190/ By Troy Nankervis Friday 17th Feb 2017

SECTION TWO

VERBAL ABUSE

Sometimes the abuser uses intimidating verbal abuse and language, to strike fear into the heart of his victim, in the same way that a lion roars before it attacks its prey. The prey is so afraid that it loses all power of reason. It becomes paralyzed and literally defeated in the presence of its great enemy, before the lion even pounces.

- Does he abuse you, shouting loudly even when the children are around?

- Are you constantly belittled and told its all your fault, and that you're no good?

- Are you told that you are stupid, worthless, and does he call you dummy?

- Are you shouted at, and made to feel as if you don't have a brain of your own?

- Are you called critical and disrespectful names and utterly humiliated in private as well as in public?

SECTION THREE

EMOTIONAL ABUSE

This takes place when you are being controlled in the relationship by being emotionally blackmailed. When you are made to feel as if you have no choice in anything, especially if you are to be allowed to remain in a relationship with your partner. When he makes you feel as if it's your job to make and keep him happy, even if that involves detriment to your own soul and happiness.

When your 'no' is not, good enough, respected or even heard, this is emotional abuse. Every human being has the right to have an opinion, and a viewpoint. Everyone is therefore entitled to express themselves, without having the fear of repercussion. Alarm bells therefore should always start to go off, if you are being restrained and greatly restricted in any way.

When other people impose their will over yours, when they feel their rights are more important than yours, you need to know that this is not healthy, and something is definitely not right! This is not a good setup! The truth is that you don't have to accept this as your lot in life. You don't have to roll over and be a door mat, accepting it as the only reality possible.

- Why should you be resigned to allowing others to violate you?

- Why is it alright for them to feel they can?

- Why do you allow other people to do that to you?

When you are told ...

"I will love you if ..."

"I will stop loving you if ..."

"If you really loved me you would do X ... Y ... Z."

When you are made to feel as if love will be withdrawn, because the abuser's conditions are not being met, then you should know that this can never be real love, and it is at this point that you need to realize that your well-being is at stake big time!

When he threatens to hurt or kill himself if you don't do what he says or wants, he is manipulating and emotionally abusing you. This is usually a sure sign of things to come, and an indication that things will inevitably escalate, into abuse including physical aggression and violence at some point.

I remember being on duty one evening and a lady that had recently moved into the refuge came into the office to see me. I handed her a letter that had arrived for her in the post. She looked at it, then at me, then she burst into tears! When I asked her what was wrong, she said, "I am crying because this is the first time I have ever been allowed to open my own post! It is very emotional for me because I have never had the experience before!" I must admit I was truly stunned by her admission, and by the reality of how domestic violence violates people's rights, on the most basic of levels!

Truthfully if you know what to look for, there are usually tell-tale signs. So domestic violence does not need to be something that creeps up on you! If you are not however adequately informed and aware, it is possible to miss all the clues until it is too late. Before long the first punch, kick, or slap is thrown, before you even get a chance to take it all in!

Love is something that was meant to be given freely. When you receive and give it, this process is supposed to be one that sets you heart free to soar like an eagle! True love is not supposed to put you in chains and make you feel as if there is some kind of a noose or yoke around your neck! (Metaphorically speaking). This completely defeats the object!

A good and healthy relationship therefore should empower you, instead of leaving you feeling helpless, hopeless, depressed and trapped! A good and healthy relationship is not characterized by someone always playing 'mind games,' to the point that you never know whether you are coming or going.

When your partner calls you degrading names, humiliates you, puts you down all the time, making you feel as small as possible at every opportunity, this is emotional abuse. When they get a kick out of degrading you and stripping you of all dignity, when they make you feel as if you are sub human or less, in public and private, emotional abuse is at its best!

You are being emotionally abused when you are blamed for everything that goes wrong. When you are intimidated into doing things that you would not ordinarily do, if you had the choice. When you are made to feel as if you are worth nothing, as if you are totally inadequate in every area, and not even worth loving ... this is emotional abuse!

- Does he cry, apologize, and behave as if he's truly sorry for what he did to you, each time he does it?

- Do you melt and go all gooey at the sight of his tears?

- Has it ever crossed your mind that they could very well be crocodile tears?

- Is it possible that this has become nothing more to him than a game and a senseless habit?

- Does he swear it will never happen again?

- Do you feel you still desperately love the man who hurts you?

- Even if you managed to physically separate yourself from him, do you still feel compelled to have contact, whether that is by phone, text or other social media avenues?

- Does he tell you he loves you so much, as if that is supposed to wipe the slate clean and make everything alright?

- Does he throw tantrums to get his own way?

- Does he use the threat of killing himself to blackmail you?

- Does he manipulate the kids, buying them things in an effort to confuse them and turn them against you?

- When you are isolated from family and friends, made to feel completely alone, and as if the threat of harm looms over you, you are obviously less likely to fight for your rights. Your abuser   takes full advantage of his position of power, knowing that he has you right where he wants you.

- Do family and friends seem uncomfortable and shocked when you share scenarios of what it is like at home?

- Are friends and family afraid for you?

- Does he go as far as even threatening your family members if you don't do what he wants?

- Do you make excuses for his bad attitude and disgusting behaviour, including the shocking way he treats you?

- Is he paranoid and always accusing your friends and family of looking down on him, talking about him and judging him?

- When they express concern for you, do you usually habitually just brush it aside automatically?

- Do you try to convince them that you can handle and tame him?

- Do you get nervous whenever he is around?

- Do you feel able to talk freely when he enters the room, or do you find yourself going into 'walking on egg shells mode?'

- Are you always afraid you will say the wrong thing, because from past experience you always manage to, according to him?

- Does he blame you in some perverse way for his own unacceptable behaviour? Does he say things like, "now look what you made me do?"

- Does he blame you for making him upset and angry?

- Do you apologize for things that you're not even guilty of, just to try in vain to keep the peace and not make him angry?

- Instead of accepting responsibility for his own behaviour, does he try to deflect the blame from himself, where it rightfully should go, on to you? Does he do this by distracting from the main issues?

- Does he blame everyone but himself for the problems within the relationship?

The truth is that you are not responsible for someone else's behaviour. What you choose to do about it however, will determine what happens at the end of your story. You can certainly decide how to react to the way you are being treated and put a stop to such abuse once and for all! It does not actually matter how powerless you may have been made to feel, the reality is that you are the one who does have the power to change things. It will not be easy, but it is possible, with the right help and support.

- Does he successfully make you feel frightened and as if you are in danger, every minute of every day? If he does, you are being emotionally abused.

- Is he so controlling that he makes you feel as if he literally owns you, successfully controlling every area of your life?

- Does he take it to such levels, that he actually believes he has the right, to determine even what and when you and your children eat?

- Do you ever catch yourself telling others, "he would not put up with that!"

- Does he say things like, "If it's good enough for me then it is good enough for you and anyone else around here!"

- Does he check up on you every chance he gets?

- Does he watch the clock and time you when you have been out?

- Does he interrogate you with twenty questions about where you have been when you return?

- Does he ask you who you have been with, or spoken to?

- Does he accuse you falsely of having an affair?

- Does he force you to have sex, even in front of the children?

- Does he blame everything and everyone except himself?

- If you go out anywhere, does he ring and text you so much that you feel you might as well be at home with him?

- Does he stare you out and intimidate you, into backing down at every opportunity he gets?

- Would he rather scrounge off you than get a job?
- Does he manipulate you by withholding necessities like money and food?
- Has he ever wounded you by being unfaithful to you?
- Has he ever forced you into prostitution and then taken the money?
- Do you feel owned by him as if you are his property?

If and when he does these things, he is taking away your power of choice. On the one hand it humiliates you, and at the same time it makes him feel even more powerful. As far as he is concerned, he is a legend in his own mind, so this sort of behaviour reinforces his fantasy, 'that he is king of the world!'

Whenever you find the one who is supposed to protect, love and care for you the most, is actually the same person who is attacking, threatening and frightening you, this can be incredibly confusing and particularly painful. It is disheartening and soul destroying to say the least, and difficult to see any reason to pick yourself up and be encouraged. With all the available help out there however, that is exactly what you must do! (We will look at a useful list of contacts in a later chapter) (Page 123).

Amira had been married to her ex-husband Imran for sixteen years. Apparently, Imran drank a lot. He had promised to stop drinking the year before, but this never materialized. Whenever he was drunk, things escalated, and he was even more nasty than usual. On top of that, he taught the kids to lie by his example.

Tensions had been rising steadily over the years, so one

night she had an argument with him over a remote control. He spat at her with contempt as he verbally abused her. He pushed her and threatened that he would not allow her to run away, but that she was going to die by his hands. At the end of the evening, he changed his mind and told her to leave, even though she had nowhere to go!

The following morning, Amira asked (Imran who drives) to take their son to schools. Their son went to a different school from their daughters, and Amira obviously couldn't take all the children to where they needed to be, by herself. Imran refused to help at all. Amira took her son to school by train, but inevitably he got there very late unfortunately.

A little later on that day, Amira received a call from her son's school. She couldn't talk then because her husband was in the room. When she went to collect him at home time, she was called into the office. She was informed that her son had been very upset at school. She was told that he had disclosed that his dad had pushed him down the stairs and hit him in the head. At this point, Amira was then given two options. She was told that if she went home, all of her children would be taken into foster care. (They had already been down this road before and had been very unhappy). She was also told that the other option was for her and the children to go into a place of safety. She chose the latter, and she and the children were then accompanied to a refuge. Social services also got involved to offer the family support.

SECTION FOUR

FINANCIAL ABUSE

- Does he keep very tight reins on you financially?
- Does he then complain bitterly when you don't have enough money to cook a decent meal?
- Does he run up bills in your name?

If the answers to these questions are yes, then this is when the control over your life is of a financial nature. You may indeed be entitled to money that you never see or get your hands on, because this is what your abuser has decided. Even if a bank account is in your name, you may still be denied access, to the money that is rightfully yours. You may be forced to work and then your wages are taken away from you. Alternatively, you may not be allowed to work, for fear that having your own money would enable you to be more independent.

Financial abuse takes place when you are forced to beg for money, to buy basic much needed things like food, soap, things for the children and other personal items. When you find yourself in the position where your abuser believes there is no reason why he should not commit fraud, or theft against you, you are without a doubt, being financially abused.

SECTION FIVE

SEXUAL ABUSE

This takes place when the victim is forced to participate in sexual acts. This includes being forced to have sexual intercourse against your will, which amounts to being raped. It can include being touched when you do not want to be touched, as well as being forced to touch them when you don't want to. When you are being forced to sell your body and receive unwanted attention from them, making you feel cheap, you are being sexually abused.

Sexual abuse can be one or the most devastating forms of abuse for the person involved. Perhaps one of the reasons is because sex is always meant to take place, within the context of a loving relationship between consenting adults. Whenever this therefore takes place violently, and against the victims will, (typically characteristic of when rape takes place), it is not only traumatic, but it is also soul destroying. It often encompasses all the other forms of abuse simultaneously, such as physical, mental, and verbal, which makes it particularly effective. The victim is left with the feeling of once again being pathetically defeated. There is often little hope that things will ever change, when all dignity and respect is lost at such a basic human level. The victim feels violated and powerless, as the abuser forcefully takes what he wants, knowing that it is not freely or willingly given. The victim is forced to participate in unwanted sexual activity, because as far as the abuser is concerned, the victim's choice is an irrelevant consideration!

For the victim however, this is a complete nightmare which they can't seem to wake up from. They feel dirty and guilty that they allowed this atrocity to happen to them. At the same time, they feel that they were completely powerless to have stopped it from taking place. They often blame themselves and are tormented by thoughts that perhaps, they should have done things differently, screamed louder, and fought back harder.

Sexual abuse can occur just because the victim is being forced and manipulated into watching pornographic material. Abuse comes into play when the victim's right to choose has been snatched away.

Michelle Thompson an MP for Edinburgh West, shared her experience of been attacked and raped, when she was only fourteen years old. She was a victim of someone she knew. She talked about what she went through and how the experience made her feel. She decided to share publicly about her ordeal in parliament. She said it was because as an MP, she wanted to give a voice to people who are unable to speak out in the same way. She really wants the focus to be on effecting change for many other women, who still suffer in silence.

END NOTES

1. https://www.independent.co.uk/news/uk/politics/michelle-thompson-rape-age-14-account-story-video-speaker-john-bercow-cry-tears-a7463786.html By Jon Stone 8th of Dec 2016

PSYCHOLOGICAL (MENTAL ABUSE)

This type of abuse certainly highlights and supports all the other forms of abuse making them possible. Usually the abuser systematically wears down the victim mentally over time, grooming them long before they ever even throw the first punch.

Mental abuse occurs when the abuser continually plays mind games with the victim, literally toying with them just because they can. When the harassment they are responsible for, happens to such a tremendous extent that the victim can no longer distinguish between what is in fact reality, and what is not, this is mental abuse. The abuser has so mastered the art of manipulating the victim, that they begin controlling even their very thinking process. It is as if they are literally in their head and able to pull their invisible strings. The victim is then resigned to dancing to the beat of whatever music their abuser decides to play at any given time!

At times Robert would cleverly get into my head and stop me in my tracks just by sending me a text message! I remember once he told me, "You have become completely insignificant in people's lives! Where are all the people who are supposed to love you?" It was a question strategically asked and one pregnant with meaning. As I pondered the answer, I felt so intimidated by him that I almost didn't remember what it felt like to not be bullied by him. He had no problem getting me to believe that it was all my fault.

Even when we were not physically together, we might as well have been, the way that I was affected and left feeling.

Regardless of time and distance, he had the ability to send me somewhere mentally, and ruin my whole day just by something he said. He had such incredible power over me unfortunately. After two years of wearing me down, if he had told me the sky was pink with white spots, I would have believed him. It was only later that I learned and came to understand that the power he had over me was in fact power I had naively given to him. I also learned later, that no other human being, is qualified or deserves to ever have that much power over me!

A young lady called Baljit found herself in quite a dilemma, as things certainly had not worked out, or gone the way she had planned. She was in her late twenties, married and the mother of three children under five. She found herself to be in a nightmare that she could not seem to wake up from, no matter what she did.

It all started when she met Jaswinder. Although they were both from Asian backgrounds, it was by no means an arranged marriage. It was in fact quite the opposite. They met at university, fell in love and decided to get married. They both had good jobs and the plan therefore, was to save up enough money to buy their own place.

Jaswinder's parents however had other ideas. They persuaded them to move in and live with them, so that they had the opportunity to save and get together enough of a deposit, to buy their place sooner. Of-course the young couple were grateful and thought it was a brilliant idea. They were excited that they would be able to save even faster than they originally thought possible. They set about making their plans.

Once they got married however and moved into the family home, the mother in law became very aggressive towards Baljit, and demanding of them as a couple. She immediately set about showing her true colors and laying down the law. She told them that they no longer needed to buy their own place. After all they were now living with them and had a suitable roof over their head!

On top of that while she was on a roll, she demanded they begin to pay her six hundred pounds every month for the privilege of living there. She also got on their case demanding they start a family so that she could have grandchildren! The young couple on the other hand, had planned to wait before starting a family. They wanted to concentrate on getting a mortgage first.

When Baljit spoke to Jaswinda privately about using contraceptives, he adamantly refused explaining that they were not allowed to because of the family's religion! He caved in to the pressure obviously deciding that his mother's wrath was far worse than his wife's. Baljit was besides herself with frustration.

As a result, before long Baljit became pregnant and had a son. Not long after he was born, before she knew what was going on, she found she was pregnant again and then again in very quick succession. Suddenly she went from being a busy woman with a good job, to a mother of three small children. She had no choice but to give up work to look after the kids. This was not a good set up or situation. This was definitely not how she planned it! On top of everything else she got absolutely no help to look after the kids, and she was expected to do endless chores around the house.

Her mother in law cracked the whip and made it seem as if her mission in life was to make her daughter in law's life a living hell. It later came out that apparently her issue with Baljit, was that she had planned how she was going to get her son to marry a nice 'yes' girl from Pakistan. At the same time her son Jaswinder rebelled and burst her bubble because he put his foot down, absolutely refusing to marry anyone the family chose from Pakistan. To rub salt in the wound, of course Baljit came along and destroyed her elaborate plan. This was definitely something she intended to make her pay for, the rest of her life!

The mental and emotional abuse became a way of life therefore for Baljit. She had no money of her own anymore, so her independence was truly a thing of the past. Presently she had her work cut out as she looked after the kids, the husband, the in laws, cooked, cleaned and became essentially a live-in slave. Baljit was trapped but could not do a thing about it. Jaswinder her husband, could not really do a lot to help her because he found himself working every hour God sent, to pay his mother the money she demanded. He felt his hands were tied, and that he had no choice either!

Amadia an eighteen year old Nigerian woman, with a six month old baby, initially arrived in the United Kingdom unaccompanied. The home office however managed to track down the man she referred to as her 'brother.' It was arranged for her to live with him, his wife, and three children, babysitting for them most of the time. This however was not a good set up, as the wife was very suspicious of her. This made her hostile, aggressive and cold towards Amadia. Meanwhile, her brother who was supposed to provide for her and the baby, in reality, only saw to their bare essentials. Whenever he was home she had to stay in her room because she was not allowed to sit in the same room as him! She was forced to cook and clean for the family. The health visitor had concerns about the young lady and her child, as the story began to unfold. The child's father was apparently a friend of Amadia's brother.

Sadly, in 2016 a man named Lance hart ended up killing his wife Claire and daughter Charlotte before he killed himself. This happened just days after the marriage ended and she left him and moved into a new property. Their two sons Luke and Ryan were out of the country at the time and were therefore not attacked by him.

In the family home, Lance was not usually physically abusive. In fact the abuse was mainly mental and emotional, so it wasn't easily spotted by the professionals involved with the family, namely the GP. The family didn't go to the police because they didn't know that what they were going through was illegal. They were not aware that the law had been changed, so that someone could be convicted for coercive controlling behaviour.

Ryan told the BBC "No-one knew what to look for. Unfortunately, it was missed by us and we lived it."

Luke said, "We were living a personal hell and our father was dangerous. I think a lot of people felt afraid of asking us what was going on because of the fear he had cultivated, especially around close family. They were all afraid of helping us because of that fear."

Now the brothers are campaigning for a greater awareness of coercive controlling behaviour, so that other families don't have to go through what they had to.

END NOTES

1. https://www.bbc.co.uk/news/uk-england-lincolnshire-46387407 29th of November 2018

SECTION SEVEN

HONOUR BASED ABUSE

There have been many crimes committed against women all over the world. In fact, more than eleven thousand such crimes have been committed, and recorded between 2010 and 2014 according to the police force in the United Kingdom. The justification for these guilty perpetrators has always been supposedly to protect and defend the honour of the family involved. Apparently, they believe their reputation is somehow at stake, and that they have not been shown in a favourable light. Suddenly as far as they are concerned there is a major issue, concerning a daughter, wife, or daughter-in-law. (Basically, the woman involved), has somehow brought terrible shame on the family. This is usually because she has chosen to disobey them, doing things her way, in spite of family disapproval and threats. As far as they are concerned, it becomes inevitable that such a woman must be made to pay for this. This kind of rebellion and bravado must be stamped out and completely eradicated. After all they certainly do not want any other women inspired to follow their example and get any ideas about breaking free. The family's tattered reputation must be restored at all cost! In this kind of scenario, nothing is too high a price to pay, even if that means committing cold blooded murder!

An honour killing therefore amounts to when a murder is committed by the family of the victim. In their opinion, she is guilty of crimes such as failing to enter a marriage they have chosen, going off and getting her own boyfriend, (made worse if he is not of their religion or cast.

Honour violence is when a woman is brutally beaten up, taught a lesson which may even lead to death! As far as the family are concerned she has brought shame on the family reputation and honour.

Often it is characteristic of honour killing and violence to be carried out by the victim's own family, (parents, brothers, uncles, mothers, sisters). They entertain a firm belief that the family honour is worth protecting at all cost. They don't take kindly, to their women folk adopting 'westernized' ways of thinking, as opposed to their more traditional customs and ways of doing things.

Occasionally a young lady has been able to involve the police and make a great escape just in the nick of time. If and when this happens, she will often have to enter the 'witness protection scheme,' which will involve changing her complete identity. The hope is that this will make it harder for her to be found. This however doesn't stop them from searching for her! She will unfortunately, also have to move away from all she knows and all that is familiar. It is very drastic and traumatic, but sometimes the only way to keep her safe, from people who will kill if the opportunity presents itself. These are extreme circumstances.

ANEESA'S STORY

Aneesa was from Birmingham in the West Midlands. She was in her early twenties and very close to her mother, especially as she had recently lost her father. As a result of the death of her dad, her brother assumed the role of 'man of the house.' Before her dad died, he had arranged a marriage for her, with a man from Pakistan. It was however a marriage of convenience. Aneesa and her new husband lived completely separate lives. In fact, her husband used her just to get into the United Kingdom. Once married, they hardly had anything to do with one another.

Aneesa had a boyfriend of her own and got pregnant. When her brother found out about the boyfriend and pregnancy, he saw it as his duty to kill her for 'dishonouring,' the family name so he smothered her with a pillow. He was convicted of manslaughter and got five years. He claimed he was just trying to frighten her and didn't mean to kill her!

At the refuge I often got chatting to the ladies and girls about their personal journey. It always helped to know where they were coming from, to get a better understanding of how best to steer them in the right direction. Many of them from Asian backgrounds often confessed, that they were mostly severely restricted at home. They were not allowed to go anywhere without a chaperone, not allowed to wear western cloths, or choose their own educational path, career or life partner!

Subsequently the women apparently guilty of bringing shame on the family were often effectively dealt with unfortunately, by killing them. The requirements of each family involved, varies from family to family, but the essential elements are the same. It is about control and manipulation and using brute force to exert the right, to dominate their victims.

There seems to be a problem with people tied up heavily in culture and tradition. (They seem steeped so deep in what they believe, that they cannot comprehend that their daughter who by all accounts may have been born in a western country), obviously does not share their beliefs, and actually has different beliefs on many key issues. These women are punished for doing so by the family, for not complying, and daring to be 'wilfully disobedient!'

Usually when the family members are carrying out greatly orchestrated strategies, to keep the victim 'controlled,' they often go to great lengths to cover their tracks. This could and often does include, apparently co-operating with the police, feigning sorrow and regret if ever caught in the act of violence, or if the daughter seeks help from the authorities.

Kamila suffered much physical and emotional abuse from her husband and 'the family,' for many years. She ended up needing to see a psychiatrist because all the abuse had affected her greatly, making her very depressed.

Initially when she and her husband first got married, things were alright. After a few years however, he suddenly began to accuse her repeatedly of having an affair. Things got so bad between them that she left him and went into a refuge.

She had not been there long when 'the family,' persuaded her to return home. They promised things would change and they would give her far more support. She expressed reservation because her husband had recently married someone else (a new wife, with whom he had a child).

They reassured her however, and she agreed to go home. Things did not work out and Kamila decided she wanted a divorce. They wouldn't hear of it, or allow her to file for a divorce, as that would bring shame on the family. They persuaded her instead to have a break especially as she had been suffering from depression. They arranged for her to go to family members in Pakistan. When she got there, they seized her passport. They held her against her will and would not allow her to return home to the United Kingdom.

She was in Pakistan for eighteen months in all. During that time, her health deteriorated, and she lost three and a half stones. Eventually they decided to send her back to the UK, because they had run out of ideas about what to do with her. When she returned eventually, she ran away and went back into a refuge. She knew from experience that this was the only way to escape the inevitable abuse from the family.

Honour abuse often includes emotional, physical, and mental abuse, as well as deception. It works because the community within which it takes place all work together, keeping secrets and vital evidence hidden. It has been known to end in kidnapping, beatings and eventually murder in many cases.

To read a real-life story and an example of honour based abuse, read the book I wrote called *The Only Arranged Marriage* the authorized biography of Raj Jarrett.'

SECTION EIGHT

FEMALE GENITAL MUTILATION

Female genital mutilation is essentially the circumcision of girls, that can take place from an infant age, right up to a girl's teenage years. The children involved have no choice in the matter. They are emotionally manipulated and physically abused by the people they love and trust the most, which is what makes it all the more horrific! These same people unfortunately are determined to make the Genital mutilation happen. This cannot be taken lightly or watered down to make it sound better! It is what it is, and this is nothing short of child abuse!

It is usually carried out by older female members of the young person's family, including mothers, aunties, and grandmothers. It is done in the name of 'tradition,' and is passed down from one generation to the next. Each of these women suffered as a child as they all had it done to them. Now as far as they are concerned, it is their turn to execute the same deed on these poor innocent unsuspecting children!

As the name suggests, the act involves deliberately mutilating, injuring, cutting and disfiguring the genitals of these little girls. It is incredibly painful and can and often does include sewing up the vagina to make it smaller. The job is never done hygienically or with any anaesthesia, because the women responsible are just ordinary people with no medical training. As a result, it is often inevitably accompanied by infections, and major blood loss!

The trauma these girls experience understandably causes horrendous problems to their health and wellbeing. They subsequently suffer terribly during sex, and experience chronic pain. They can actually die during childbirth, because of all the complications that can and often do arise.

On the first of February 2019, the first conviction for FGM was secured. A woman from East London, was found guilty and convicted for mutilating her three year old little girl!

Lynette Woodrow, of the Crown Prosecution Service, said: "We can only imagine how much pain this vulnerable young girl suffered and how terrified she was. A three-year-old has no power to resist or fight back.

"Her mother then coached her to lie to the police, so she wouldn't get caught but this ultimately failed. We will not hesitate to prosecute those who commit this sickening offence."

For help with this issue contact:

FGM Helpline: 0800 0283550

Contact: fgmhelp@nspcc.orh.uk

END NOTES

1. https://www.cps.gov.uk/london-north/news/mother-first-be-convicted-female-genital-mutilation 1st of Feb 2019

HUMAN TRAFFICKING

WHAT IS HUMAN TRAFFICKING?

Definition: Human trafficking is the crime of moving people illegally, often to a different country, so they can be forced to have sex for money, or to work for little or no money. (Macmillan Dictionary) 2009.

As the definition suggests, trafficking involves trading human beings, and exploiting them for material gain and profit, just as if they were products or goods! These people are taken advantage of by traffickers who consider them to be weak and vulnerable. The abusers use their power to oppress, enslave, and exploit those who cannot defend, protect or stand up and fight for themselves.

This can include children who have been groomed for the purpose, as well as vulnerable adults. It is a complete setup and often involves kidnapping, and everything that violates the free will of a human being, including forcing them to take drugs! It is characteristic of the crime of trafficking to be about personal gratification of the abuser. Sexual abuse is usually therefore involved, especially when the victims involved are not in a position to defend themselves, fight back or put an end to what is happening to them!

Sometimes trafficking is about making money through child labour. The stronger, abuse their victims, by using their 'power and control,' to dominate and prey on the vulnerable. The people who are being trafficked are forced to work in sweatshops sewing clothes, or in catering, cooking food from sunrise to sun down. They are helpless victims and have no choice but to do as they are told or face the devastating consequences!

SIGNS OF HUMAN TRAFFICKING

Someone who has been involved in human trafficking would no doubt display some, or all of the following characteristics:

Many of them are withdrawn and fearful around other people. Considering the terrible things, they have no doubt experienced, this is totally understandable. It is extremely difficult for them to be able to trust others easily. Every time they have chosen to trust someone in the past, they have been used, abused and let down. It is therefore no surprise that they often conclude that trust is too high a price to pay! Subsequently, they become insecure as they have never experienced any stability in their lives.

Children who have been victims of trafficking, become severely traumatized by being violently removed from their families often by force. Bearing the circumstances in mind it is highly unlikely that it would have been possible for them, to have had adequate opportunity to get a good and consistent education, or a normal childhood for that matter.

Apart from the obvious things like physical bruises and scars, they will quite possibly also suffer from mental health issues like depression, eating disorders and the tendency to self-harm as well. They may also display inappropriate sexual behaviour towards others. They are often unaccustomed to and unfamiliar with proper boundaries, because of what has been done to them. Sexually transmitted diseases, unwanted, unplanned pregnancies as well as the challenge of abortions, are also issues that the victims of trafficking must often deal and cope with.

Such people may have a classic fear of the dark. They can

often turn out to be quite aggressive, towards others as they are forced to do whatever is necessary for self-preservation reasons. The things they have experienced will often have been accompanied by violence, so they learn to be that way too. They can and often do find themselves addicted to drugs, which makes it impossible for them to easily break free from the ones who hold them captive! The setup is strategic on the part of their abusers.

If you are affected by this issue and need help contact:

Modern Slavery helpline: 0800 0121700

SECTION TEN

FORCED MARRIAGE

Marriage is supposed to be all about the coming together of two compatible people, who are in love and have equally chosen and decided to be together. The achievement of such a union, should be the beginning of a rapturous joy that is difficult to even describe and completely contagious to everyone else around them!

Forced marriage is the total opposite as the name suggests. Usually in this scenario, one or both people are forced by family members to embark upon the journey of marriage that neither of them want. It is typical that the unfortunate couple, have no say or choice in the matter. It is however what the family have decided is going to happen and that is the end of it.

A forced marriage is therefore possible, through the sheer force of using and exerting a pressure cooker like state of affairs. Abuse is the vehicle used to violate the will of the couple and remove their freedom of choice.

For help with this issue contact:

Phone: 0800 5999247

Contact: www.karmanirvana.org.uk/

Email: fmu@fco.gov.uk

FCO FORCED MARRIAGE UNIT

Phone:0207 0080151 or 00442070080151 if calling from abroad.

SECTION ELEVEN

STALKING

This occurs when the victim is forced to endure completely unwanted attention from someone who displays totally obsessive, 'out of control' behaviour. It involves the stalker harassing and intimidating the victim at every opportunity. This is usually by disrespecting, all their boundaries and pushing them to the absolute limit.

The stalker often believes they have the right to physically follow them, phone them all the time, and basically go to a lot of trouble to invade their privacy and disrupt their world. This is very much about the stalker exerting control over and exercising power over their victim. They do this by regularly unnerving them, using fear as the vehicle.

Stalking could start simply because someone has mistakenly misinterpreted and misunderstood when a person is being friendly towards them. There is a crossing of wires as suddenly the stalker becomes literally obsessed, bombarding their victim with unwanted texts, phone calls and visits. They also invest a lot of time and effort spying on them! They become pushy and refuse to leave the person alone or show them any kind of respect. Essentially, they refuse to take no for an answer!

The stalker's aim is to seriously violate their victims by invading their personal space, at every possible opportunity they get, causing major distress, and leaving them feeling threatened and ultimately afraid. The victim feels very uncomfortable whenever the stalker is around, becoming nervous and unable to relax, always looking over their shoulder, finding it impossible to avoid being on edge.

Stalkers also like to destroy their victim's property. Smashing up their things gives the stalker a sense of power because it is a way of controlling them. Stalking can be part of a domestically violent scenario, and in very serious cases, it can unfortunately even lead to serious harm where the victim is killed.

Molly Mclaren ended her relationship with Joshua Stimpson because he was obsessive. Twelve days after they split up, he began to stalk her. She was concerned enough to confront him about it. She also shared this concern with her mother, and a friend.

One day she went to the gym, and he turned up there. Shortly afterwards he apparently left but in fact waited for her outside. Unsuspecting she went and sat in her car. Before she realised what was happening, he forcefully opened her car door, and violently attacked her. He cut her throat and stabbed her 75 times in all. It was obvious that he was determined to kill her. She lost her life as he did. He was charged and given a life sentence with a minimum of 26 years.

NETWORK FOR SURVIVING STALKING

National stalking helpline: 08088020300

Contact: www.stalkinghelpline.org

Email: advice@stalkinghelpline.org

Or use the contact form that can be found here:

https://www.suzylamplugh.org/contact-the-helpline

END NOTES

1. https://thetab.com/uk/2018/02/07/the-case-of-molly-
   mclaren-stabbed-75-times-by-her-ex-for-breaking-up-
   with-him-60303 By Josh Kaplan

The Effects Of Domestic Violence

PART ONE

THE EFFECTS OF DOMESTIC VIOLENCE ON WOMEN

Domestic violence is such a destructive force. As such it has a terrible and devastating effect on women in absolutely every way. It goes so much deeper than just the obvious and the physical damage done. A woman will often find that psychologically and emotionally she has also been affected by the abuse. It is inevitable that she is changed forever by her experience. It is therefore often quite a long road to recovery, on so many levels. This is certainly the case, when you consider all the various issues that may arise out of all that she has been through. These things as challenging and difficult as they may prove to be, must be dealt with and overcome. This applies especially if there is to be life after domestic violence! With adequate signposting to relevant agencies and professional help, it is possible to get life back on track, and for that life to be great again.

A woman who has been through the unfortunate experience of domestic violence can quite easily and understandably develop mental health issues, so here is an overview of some of the issues that she may be affected by including the following:

BAD NERVES

It is not surprising that such a woman will often become extremely jumpy. The slightest noise, sudden movements, meeting new people, all these things suddenly become a massive insurmountable challenge for her because of the previous trauma she has experienced. Her nerves are no longer what they used to be.

When she has become accustomed to looking over her shoulder, watching her p's and q's, and desperately trying her best not to upset the apple cart, this becomes her 'norm.' Suddenly the goal and driving force of her life becomes avoiding anything that will 'set off her abuser,' and make him lose the plot! It is not surprising then that she may very well suffer from bad nerves, as she develops the habit of constantly compromising herself, just to survive. After all this is a most unnatural way to have to live!

ANXIETY AND PANIC ATTACKS

Anxiety and panic attacks are a common challenge that victims of domestic violence find themselves becoming familiar with, as they struggle to overcome devastating effects. When forced to live in a constant heightened state of fear, and when this underlines most of your decisions and the way you are made to live your life, it becomes very difficult to operate apart from fear. Fear becomes the root and core of most things. Suddenly it becomes near impossible to separate what you do, and who you are, from the power that fear has over you.

INSOMNIA

Some of the women I worked with suffered from insomnia, and sometimes needed sleeping tablets to be able to get through each night. Being in their own particular abusive situation, meant that often the cover of night made their situation worse. This was often the time they were attacked, made to feel most vulnerable, and tormented the most. Sometimes the only way to survive was to stay awake, because their minds came to understand that sleep spelt 'danger.' So as this became a regular pattern, then even when physically away from the situation and in a safe place, (in the refuge for instance), sleep had now become a big problem, and something that evaded them. Finding themselves physically out of the situation had not made enough of a significant difference to their minds, to make them feel a whole lot better. The truth is that although physically they are removed from the threatening situation, they have unfortunately grown accustomed to, things feeling desperately bad. They do not feel better, because psychologically they are still living in a time warp!

DEPRESSION

Depression is often another side effect of coming through the domestically violent scenario. When a woman has been so suppressed within the relationship, when her rights have been violated at every opportunity, and she is devalued and treated as if she is worth nothing at all, it affects her drastically. This is especially true when this has been the case over time. When she is not allowed or encouraged to express herself, she may begin to feel very low in herself. When things are not dealt with, but swept under the carpet, this is incredibly unhealthy. Just because they are temporarily buried does not mean that they have gone away and no longer have an effect. When a woman's circumstance forces her to live in denial, and to avoid rocking the boat, it becomes easier for her to clam up and go emotionally numb. This is a survival mechanism which means that she is now able to function and get on with things in a manner of speaking. The emotional pain that imprisons her is ever present, but not necessarily at the forefront of things, or even obvious to the people around her. This however does not make it any less deadly. In fact, often the strain on the woman's health begins to show. She may develop other mental health issues also as a result.

EATING DISORDERS

Sometimes a woman may develop an eating disorder as a direct result of suffering from domestic violence. As she is often subject to her abuser's controlling behaviour, the chances are that she is left feeling helpless and that her choices have been violated and restricted. This can cause her to feel as if she must have something that she still has some control over. This can therefore set her on a path where she develops a very unhealthy relationship with food. Instead of eating well and in a balanced manner, she may become obsessed with her food intake. Some go as far as denying themselves, hardly eating much at all. Others on the other hand go the other way and feel the need to bring new meaning to the term 'comfort eating!'

DRUGS AND ALCOHOL DEPENDENCY

Some women try to find other ways to cope with the trauma of the way their lives have turned out. They may develop a drug or alcohol dependency on one or both, as a result.

In the refuge that I worked at, this was a difficult and tough issue to constantly have to deal with. Many of the women arrived displaying different degrees of dependency. For them this had become their coping mechanism, and the way they had managed to get through their days.

In our support of them however, we were obliged to encourage them to find more appropriate ways of dealing with the horror stories that had been their lives. We sign posted them to agencies, that could help them to deal with any dependencies they had developed. At the forefront of our minds, was seeing them restored to their former glory, with health and wellbeing radiating from them on every level. Obviously in these circumstances nothing is immediate, so these women found themselves on a journey to recovery in every sense of the word.

SELF HARM:

Another issue that affects victims of domestic violence is that of 'self-harm.' They may choose to self-harm as women struggle to overcome a desperate sense of an acute sense of the loss of control of their lives and situations. The choice to self-harm is not always because the woman wants to die. Usually it is a serious cry for help. When a woman has coped with her situation, by internalizing every negative feeling, memory, and thought, then these may very well be manifested by her harming herself.

A woman explained it to me this way when I asked her... she said that when she is hurting so much and so deeply inside, it is hard to think about or focus on anything else. When she cuts herself however, she has a new hurt to focus on. The hurt she feels inside, suddenly does not seem as intense or as bad as it did, and there is temporary respite.

Self-harm is an incredibly destructive type of behaviour. Once the appetite for it has been awakened, it is not easily satisfied, and can and often does become an addiction. The self-harmer then finds themselves in the position where they feel they must regularly indulge in the act, to satisfy the drive to self-harm again.

POOR SELF/BODY IMAGE

Women who are regularly subjected to abuse, tend to have a very poor self-image and practically no self-esteem. When they are verbally abused and put down at every opportunity, it is very difficult for them to come back from this and appear to be firing from all cylinders. Often their abusers control them by telling them that they are ugly, fat, and unattractive, and stupid. After hearing it again and again, (sometimes for years), it gets into the psyche of the woman, and it becomes incredibly difficult for her to shake off and not take it on board.

LOW SELF ESTEEM

Similarly, sometimes a woman is defined not only by the things that are said to her, but also the things that are done to her, against her will. She comes to believe that there has to be something wrong with her, for things to have turned out the way they have. She may blame herself. She will quite likely lose every ounce of self-confidence she ever had. She will believe in herself less and less, becoming uncertain, unsure and nervous about most things. Simple everyday tasks become a problem and a challenge. She finds it more difficult to function on anything but autopilot. In many things she is just going through the motions, and often if you look in her eyes it looks like there is no-one at home. She is in survival mode, and although she is physically alive, her soul is slowly but surely dying, as she becomes a shadow of her former self!

SHOCK

The trauma of everything a victim has been through can cause her to go into shock, as her faculties go into overload. That could mean, physically, mentally, and emotionally, perhaps even all three. It is hardly surprising when a woman is forced to deal with more than she is designed to deal with! Her ability to function is often reduced to a bare minimum, as here she finds herself operating on auto pilot, and just going through the motions!

FEAR OF SEX

If a woman has been habitually raped, it is quite possible she may understandably develop a paralyzing fear when it comes to anything to do with sex, including the thought of having to participate in the act. Being forcefully made to have sex, often means this was probably the time she has felt most hurt and vulnerable. Understandably then it will often therefore probably take time for her to recover from the trauma of this happening to her. Sometimes she may even need counselling, to assist her to deal with the mental and emotional effects the experience has had on her. The fact that she will feel as if she has no choice in the matter is one thing, but when this is accompanied by violent sexual attacks as well, it makes it even more devastating for her.

SEXUALIZATION

The effects of domestic violence can also cause things to go to the other extreme. A woman may deal with things by expressing intentional sexual undertones not in a natural sense, but rather she goes over the top in her sexual pursuits. In many ways it may indeed be her way of taking back the control she feels she has lost, and doing things on her terms instead. It is almost as if she feels the need to conquer rather than continue to be conquered!

MISCARRIAGE

For some reason there are times when a pregnant woman finds, that the domestic violence she is subjected to, seems to escalate during this most vulnerable time. As a result, she may very well suffer from a miscarriage and lose her baby.

UNWANTED PREGNANCY

A woman who has been a victim of domestic violence and who has been raped, may find herself in a position, where she is left having to cope with a pregnancy that she does not want. She faces the challenge of knowing she is carrying a baby conceived against her will, and through a violent act. This obviously puts her in an impossibly difficult position.

STRESS

A victim of domestic violence has endless reasons to be stressed out big time. By virtue of what it is, and the way it forces its victims to live in the grasp of its tight clutches, it is a serious cause of stress on every level. There is no time or opportunity to relax as the victim is understandably living on the edge, looking over their shoulder, and always trying desperately not to upset the apple cart. That in itself causes stress, and a never-ending impossible situation of catch twenty-two.

FEAR OF PHYSICAL CONTACT

A woman may very well become very uncomfortable and develop a fear of any kind of physical contact. This may occur especially, as a vast majority of the physical contact she would likely have experienced, would have been accompanied by violent assault, as fear was used to control her. It may be very difficult for her to overcome this although it is possible in time, with the right help.

FLASHBACKS

Flashbacks often occur when there has been great trauma in a person's life. During a flashback the woman usually has a sudden reoccurring powerful recollection of a past beating, rape or other violent moment. As she can never predict when she is going to have an episode, she is very fearful of the whole experience, because flashbacks do a good job of controlling her. She is always quite shaken up afterwards, as she is forced to relive the horror over and over again! She is literally experiencing a nightmare that she cannot seem to wake up from.

SUICIDAL THOUGHTS AND TENDENCIES

When a woman has been through so much that she loses all hope of things ever improving, she may start to see her only way out, as ending her life. It may not be her real desire to die, but often it is a desperate cry for help, and a desire for things to change.

PHYSICAL INJURY

Domestic violence makes physical injury highly possible, and in many cases inevitable. Sometimes the injuries are temporary and have a good chance of healing. There are those injuries however that are more permanent and long term. These are ones that occur because of consistent violence.

Examples of known injuries that can occur include painful backs, necks, shoulders, ribs, fractures, bruises, teeth that have been loosened or completely knocked out, ruptured eardrums, burns, etc.

It is typical for such a woman to wear clothing that is able to hide obvious injuries from public gaze. It becomes her aim to avoid having to answer as many questions as possible. She desperately hopes this will simplify things. She is usually afraid to tell anyone about what is really going on, in case it opens up a can of worms, that she cannot easily shut again.

MEMORY LOSS

Victims can suffer from memory loss as they struggle to come to terms with the trauma, they have been through. Many times, the victim's loss of memory is down to the need for 'self-preservation.' As the incidents that have taken place are too painful to handle, the victim finds they cannot recall certain things. What has actually happened is that the memories have been blocked from the conscious mind and pushed deep down into the sub-conscious mind. Such memories will therefore still have a grip like hold on the victim, although they may not be able to remember every single exact detail.

DEATH

The unfortunate ultimate tragic effect of domestic violence on a woman, is when she loses her battle with it and faces and succumbs to death itself.

Sian Blake was once a well-known actress in the famous

British soap *EastEnders*. At forty-three years old, she was also the mother of two sons. One was eight and the other four years old.

She had been in an on-off relationship, with the father of her children who was a violent abuser.

As Sian battled on and got older, she began to suffer from motor neurone disease and eventually became quite fragile.

Sian's sister confirmed that Sian had made the incredibly brave decision to get Christmas over with, and then leave the abusive situation she was in. She wanted more for herself and her boys, as she conceded that leaving was the only way that was ever going to happen. She never got the chance to go through with her hope and plans to break free however. She and the boys went to visit her mum just before Christmas, and that was the last time they were seen alive. There was just no sign of them after that.

The police were brought in when they were contacted by the NSPCC (The National Society For The Prevention Of Cruelty To Children). Sian's family were so worried that they also contacted the police to express their concern. They suspected that there was domestic violence going on at the hands of Sian's ex-partner.

There was unfortunately however real concern about the way the police handled things. Bearing in mind the fact that Sian's family contacted them with other initial concerns, it is difficult to understand why although Arthur Simpson (the abuser) was questioned, he was not then arrested as a result.

Sian and the children had been missing for three weeks before the police turned it from a case of just looking for missing people, to an actual murder inquiry. It was when forensics dug up the garden that they found three bodies. All three had died from head and neck injuries. In the meantime Arthur Simpson Kent had the time he needed to get his things together and leave the country. He managed to escape to Ghana but not before sending texts from Sian's phone to deceive everyone. The texts explained that she was going away for a few weeks. This was his attempt to throw people off the scent.

Time passed before he was extradited and put on trial. He was found guilty and given a life sentence. Although he had been mistaken for a family man, the reality was that he was a violent cocaine dealer and abuser. In previous relationships he was known to be violent towards even his child from a previous marriage.

Similarly, on the 28th of June 2017 Judy Malinowski died. She suffered from a horrific attack at the hands of an ex-boyfriend. He threw petrol on her and set her on fire in 2015. When she spoke about her ordeal, she explained her recollection of the moment that she was literally burnt alive. One thing she remembered vividly was 'the look of pure evil in her ex's eye!'

Her injuries were so severe that two of her fingers and both ears melted because of the sheer heat of the fire that engulfed her. 80% of her body suffered from fifth degree burns. She fought with everything she had to recover, for two years. This included her having 56 different surgeries to try to put things right, after such a horrific ordeal. She suffered from open wounds on her back and bottom, but these could not be rectified. She was just too weak to be able to lie on her stomach for this type of surgery. From her hospital bed she urged other victims of domestic violence, to get help and to run from their situation before it was too late. Eventually she unfortunately succumbed to death, leaving behind her two children. Her daughters were aged 9 &13 at the time they lost their mother.

There was also the recent story of Zoe Morgan and her boyfriend Lee Simmons who were both brutally killed by Andrew Saunders. He was Zoe's ex-boyfriend, and utterly consumed with jealousy, seemingly unable to accept that his relationship with Zoe was over. When he and Zoe were together, he was controlling and violent. This is what led to the break-up of their relationship in the first place. At first, he threatened to kill them both. He then subsequently went to where they both worked, waited for them outside, and then cold-bloodedly stabbed them one after the other.

The high-profile case of Reeva Steenkamp a model, who was killed by her boyfriend Oscar Pistorious a South African Paralympian in 2013, was all over the news. Since her death, some of her previous text messages to him have come to light which reveal quite a lot about their relationship.

"I'm scared of you sometimes and how you snap at me, and how you will react to me." (Jan 27th 2013 two and a half weeks before he shot her dead).

In another text, many things become apparent and show classic signs of an abusive relationship.

- She tried in vain to make him happy by changing her own behaviour.

- He was controlling and made her leave special social occasions early when she was having a good time, and not ready to leave yet.

- He argued loudly in public, humiliating her until she backed down.

- He consistently talked to her about his past girlfriends, and yet when she mentioned an ex-boyfriend he became angry and jealous.

- He picked on her and was 'offish,' when he was not happy about something.

- He threw tantrums.

- She couldn't be herself, neither could she please him no matter how hard she tried.

Before Reeva died she was very aware of the high figures of domestic violence against women in South Africa. She felt passionate about the subject and wanted to do something to help abused women. She was scheduled to make a speech before she was killed. It is therefore quite ironic the way she died. Jane Steenkamp (Reeva's mother) made the speech instead, to launch a foundation named after her daughter. This foundation was set up to help women and children who are victims of domestic violence since this was a cause close to Reeva's heart - https://reevasteenkampfoundation.org/ .

END NOTES

1. https://www.mirror.co.uk/news/uk-news/Sian-blake-arthur-simpson-kent-8974411 by Ben Rossington and Gemma Mullen 4th of October 2016

2. https://www.news.com.au/lifestyle/real-life/true-stories/

mumoftwo-dies-two-years-after-her-soulless-boyfriend-set-her-on-fire/news-story/8890ab91be3585 5ce73282ac77963faf June 29th 2017

3. https://news.sky.com/story/man-jailed-for-life-over-double-murder-outside-matalan-store-in-cardiff-10784992 Tuesday Feb 2017

4. https://www.independent.co.uk/news/world/africa/oscar-pistorius-trial-athlete-scared-girlfriend-reeva-steenkamp-9212563.html By Maria Tadeo n.d

PART TWO

EFFECTS OF DOMESTIC VIOLENCE ON CHILDREN

Children need consistency and to be lovingly nurtured to be able to grow into healthy young people. It is incredibly unsettling for them, (when the abuser who is an adult, and supposed to be protecting them), is behaving in a way that they cannot predict and that scares them. This makes them nervous, as they fully expect him to kick off at any time. The problem is they can never be sure exactly when it will be, as he keeps moving the goal posts. As a result, they are just constantly nervous and on edge.

Some of the children I worked with at the refuge saw things that not even adults should be subjected to. I remember the plight of one child in particular that really got to me and affected me greatly. She had been so traumatized by whatever she had witnessed, that she had gone into shock. She literally stopped talking as a result!

Domestic violence is a soul-destroying thing, for grownups so for children it is incredibly damaging indeed. The way that different children deal with it may vary, perhaps as much as every finger print varies in its uniqueness.

Of course as well as the trauma of a child witnessing violence towards its mother, it may feel guilty about this violence suffered, believing that maybe it should have done something, and could have stopped it. The child could equally have to deal with, the added trauma of having the violence directed at them by the abuser. Both scenarios are obviously very terrifying for the children involved. It can and often does leave them severely affected in one way or another.

A child may become very clingy to their mother, start wetting the bed, become a fussy and picky eater, start failing miserably at school work, become withdrawn and fail to relate adequately and appropriately to other people. They may become petrified of the dark, refusing to sleep alone or without the light on. They may appear to be confused, and always tense and stressed. They may exhibit anxiety whenever being separated from their mother during this time. (Their reasoning, perhaps their mother will be violently attacked if they are not around, or perhaps their mother will be taken away as they have already lost their father, (in spite of him being violent). These can be sure signs of a child that has been living in an atmosphere of domestic violence.

When a child finds that everything it has ever known and associated with safety, has suddenly been violently taken away, it feels insecure, unsure, unsettled, and desperately worried.

When you consider that they most likely may have had to: swap schools, adjust to life in a refuge with all its rules, get used to constantly having to look over their shoulder, get used to strangers in the form of refuge staff, social workers or even foster care, this is not an easy situation for any child to find themselves in and be forced to deal with. They often have to be put on the 'child protection register.' (This amounts to them having to be protected by the law).

In these scenarios a child should be encouraged to talk to the right people so that they don't bottle it all up inside and become a ticking time bomb. This is so important, otherwise they may grow up to be very disturbed adults, based on the terrible things they have seen and heard!

At the refuge unfortunately, some of the children inevitably, took on the persona of the abuser they had seen in action, more often, than not. Unfortunately, this had now become what was normal to them! Sometimes this involved attacking their mother hitting her, as sadly they imitated what they had seen played out before their very eyes, perhaps many, times.

Other children displayed other forms of intimidating behaviour, like staring her out, or raising their voices until she backed down, and gave into whatever demands they were making. At times the mothers would be so intimidated that they would give in to their children, just to keep the peace, and because they were afraid. Only too often unfortunately the mothers involved felt severely challenged, as they struggled to cope with the very unwelcome feelings of déjà vu.

Some of the children have had their education affected significantly. If a child has forcibly become involved in a domestically violent situation, then inevitably it will be difficult for them to be settled and secure at school, and able to focus on the business of learning!

Often their education has been affected by having to move around a lot. Learning under these circumstances often proves to be near impossible, because there are just too many other things demanding their attention and focus!

For instance, they may sometimes have to deal with the fear, that they may be kidnapped by the offending parent. If there is social services and any other agency involvement, the child has to deal with the challenge of total strangers having a say (often a big say) in what happens in their lives.

At times children affected by a home where domestic violence dominates, have justifiably a catalogue of health problems including stress, anxiety, bedwetting, nervousness, behavioural issues, insomnia, nightmares, flash backs to name just a few.

Kids can also be fearful for their own lives. In some cases, they are even threatened by the abuser, to get their mother to comply to whatever they want them to do. Some men feel there is nothing wrong with using their children as pawns, as if it were nothing more than a chess game. For them it seems, that it is all about happily abusing power, and therefore wielding it to gain an advantage. In these situations, the children's welfare and well-being seem to come very low, on their list of priorities, if they are even on that list at all!

A good example of this is one of the saddest stories I have ever heard. It was on the BBC Victoria Derbyshire show on the 20th of January 2016. She interviewed Claire Throstle an incredibly brave mother who was prepared to tell her heartbreaking, heart wrenching story.

Claire was divorced from her ex-husband Darren Sykes whom she had been married to for fifteen years. When they first got together at first everything was fine. Before long their two sons Jack and Paul, came along. For some reason Darren typically became controlling and abusive once the boys arrived. He developed a very bad temper which became frequently uncontrollable. He attended anger management classes, attempting to get things back on the right track. At the crucial moments however, the class lessons seemed completely forgotten, and failed to help much at all.

It seemed that when the kids came along his behaviour just seemed to go from bad to worse! This unfortunately actually involved him emotionally and physically abusing the boys.

In 2014 the marriage disintegrated and broke down. Claire left because as a good mum, she desperately wanted to protect her beloved children, first and foremost. This however was indeed the straw that broke the camel's back. Darren did not react very well to this new 'setup,' and it literally sent him over the edge!

As the couple were no longer together, he was only allowed limited contact with the children. This unfortunately affected him in the same way a bull loses control of itself when it sees a red cloth. Suddenly the children became much more than just pawns in a game to be played, but actually 'possessions,' to be had, because it served his selfish purposes.

Although visibly difficult for Claire during the interview, she went on to explain exactly what happened on that fateful day. The children were due to see their father after school, as this was already agreed and arranged. Jack however really was most reluctant to do so. There was hardly a bond between the boys and their father anymore, because quite frankly they were petrified of him. Understandably so, considering the things he said to them at times. He found it helpful for his cause, to tell the boys stories he'd heard about other fathers who had killed their children. Confessing to them with much emphasis, that he was sympathetic to these fathers, and actually understood why they had gone to such lengths and done what they had done.

For Claire this was the last straw. She became increasingly worried and concerned about the safety of her boys from that point on, especially whenever they were alone with him. This bothered her so much that she could no longer keep it to herself. She made a point of expressing her deep concerns to social services, and to Cafcass, (the organization that represents the voice of children).

Social services actually came out to do an assessment especially, as Paul had made a disclosure at school about something that had happened with his dad. Subsequently the contact visits were completely stopped. Claire took Darren to court because up until that point, he still had parental rights as their father. Sadly, there was a devastating outcome to the case. The court mistakenly saw the situation as no more than a custody battle between parents. It failed to see that the safety of the children involved, was in fact the very heart of the matter! As the children were still regularly going to school and academically seemed to be unaffected, the case failed to be taken as seriously as it should have been. It is obvious in hindsight that if it had been, things would have indeed turned out so differently.

During the interview, Claire continued to share about how the twenty second of October 2014 started out as just any other normal day. The boys went off happily to school as usual. They were due to have an access visit with their father after school that day. Paul was not keen and expressed to his mum the fact that he did not actually want to go. She managed to persuade him to go however, especially as at that point there was now a five hour court order in place.

Claire went to work but later on received a phone call from Cafcass. They were ringing to make her aware that she needed to keep a special eye on the boys. Apparently during the contact visit, things had kicked off and gone pear shaped. Things had not gone well as Darren had become aggressive and even barred the Cafcass officer from leaving the room at one point. (It had been a supervised visit).

Not long after Claire got home the doorbell rang. Claire's mum even commented that the boys must have come home early. Claire knew it could not be the boys because if it had been, they would have run straight into her arms. They always did that after a visit, from the sheer relief of being back home safe with their mummy. They had always seemed to be so frightened of their dad, and nervous whenever they went to see him.

When Claire went to open the door, there was a police officer standing there with a very serious look on his face. What made it worse was that the blue light was still flashing on his car, as he uttered these unforgettable words, "There's been an incident at your former home involving the boys, and there has been a fire. Claire instinctively responded, "he's done it!" The officer was not at liberty to comment at that point, so he respectfully remained silent.

Claire got to the Sheffield children's hospital and was taken to the resuscitation room where she saw Paul having CPR being done on him. The consultant regretfully informed her that they would be withdrawing treatment, as there was nothing more they could do for him.

Claire took her baby boy in her arms and held him close to her heart. Paul looked at his mum and smiled until the light went out of his eyes and he fell asleep for the last time.

Claire had to leave Paul to go to be with Jack who was in the critical burns unit in Manchester. It emerged that he had tried his very best to save his brother. He had managed to get him out of the attic and through the hatch. He was in fact still conscious when the fire officer did manage to get to him.

Five days later unfortunately Jack too succumbed to his injuries, had a cardiac arrest and also died in his mother's arms. His last words were, "My dad did this on purpose." This was his dying testament.

Following the death of the children a serious case review was carried out. The conclusion was that Darren's actions could not have been predicted. The evidence apparently that had been present at the time, had been insufficient to convince the agencies involved that Darren had posed a threat to either himself, the children, or anyone else.

Claire's answer to the findings was, "if the Cafcass officer who had to deal with Darren, felt threatened and afraid, then how did everyone think her two baby boys must have felt when having to deal with him all alone?"

Children like adults are likely to experience intense negative emotions, and are therefore affected so profoundly, that they obviously need a lot of help, support, patience, guidance, and love.

A child would struggle and have no idea how to adequately express and deal with the torrent of feelings it was experiencing, as a result of having to live with the crime of domestic violence. A child would find it difficult to understand a lot of the things it had perhaps heard, seen, and felt.

Childhood is supposed to be a carefree time in life, full of awe and wonder, where dreams come true. Childhood is certainly not supposed to be the time when children learn that this world can be a source of incredible pain, and capable of destroying dreams on every level.

A place of safety therefore is needed as soon as possible for the child. This is important to give them the best chance to develop the ability to ever trust an adult again. This is especially true, when considering it has been at the hands of adults that much suffering and hardship has been experienced.

This is the only way to undo all the damage that has been done. These are the ingredients needed to give them any chance, of becoming healthy, stable adults capable of living, normal sensible, peaceful lives in spite of any tumultuous, beginnings and backgrounds.

Just to encourage every mother out there who has ever suffered from domestic violence, you are incredibly brave! It takes immense guts to allow your protective maternal instinct, to be the thing that gives you the courage and final push, to leave the violent relationship.

The truth is that it does not really matter how young a child is, growing up in an environment where domestic violence controls and is king in the atmosphere, is not healthy. It usually will have a profound effect in one way or another as a result. The sooner a child therefore is physically, mentally, and emotionally removed from the situation, the better. Children are surprisingly resilient and with the right help and support, they can and often do bounce back from the darkest of places.

On the other hand, there are those who are so affected negatively, that they grow up to be offenders themselves. When the abuser is their only main role model, unfortunately the damage done to their delicate childish minds can sometimes be irrevocable!

There are times when social services absolutely have to get involved. Usually they will intervene, if the domestic violence is so bad that it becomes a child protection and safe guarding issue. When it gets this serious then they will offer support to the lady involved. This will sometimes include finding refuge space for the family, so that she can leave the property where the violence is taking place, with her children, and go to a place of safely. When needed, they will offer ongoing support for as long as is necessary, as far as the safety of the children is concerned.

It has been my experience working at the refuge, that in some instances there have been cases where the children have had to be removed from the mother's care. This tends to be in the most extreme and serious cases. For example, where social services have been honest enough to explain, that by refusing to leave the violent relationship, or continually returning to it after leaving, deliberately puts the children at risk. In these kind of scenarios, unfortunately, separation becomes inevitable as a result.

There were many intensely difficult moments being on duty doing a shift at the refuge. To be honest you never knew exactly what will happen, or what you will have to deal with, from one shift to the next. Bearing that in mind I have to say, that when a separation of a mother from her child becomes necessary, and social services arrive to do the deed, it is without doubt one of the most heartbreaking situations I have ever had to witness. There are no words to describe the feelings involved, neither are there any easy ways to make it happen. It is traumatic to say the least, and nothing prepares you enough to deal with it. It is not something I will forget in a hurry.

Charlize Theron (the South African actress), has been quite open about growing up in a domestic violent home as a child. Her father was often verbally abusive to her and she often witnessed her father beating up her mother.

Her situation ended dramatically when her mother felt forced to shoot her drunken, threatening, violent father, dead to protect them. That night apparently, he threatened to kill them, so Charlize's mother believed it was a choice between him or them!

Ellie Butler was six years old when she was brutally killed by her father, (the one who was supposed to be her protector)! She was murdered ten months after being returned to her parent's care following a custody battle, during which Neal and Linda Gray (her maternal grandparents) did everything they could, to fight to keep Ellie with them.

Initially she had been placed in the care of her grand-parents when she was a baby. This was because at the time, her father had been convicted of violently shaking her. This led to Ellie sustaining head/brain injuries as well as retinal injuries. Also burns to her forehead and hand were noted as other injuries she had. The conviction however was later quashed by the court of appeal, and remarkably Ellie was then returned to her parent's care. Neal and Linda Gray protested because they were concerned for her welfare, but their concerns were ignored.

The few times when Ellie was allowed to visit them, she would apparently ask her grand parents when she was coming home to live with them. As time went by, during these visits, her appearance changed for the worst. They noticed she was thin, her eyes were swollen, her clothes were dirty, and her hair was matted. This was just a shadow of the beautiful Ellie that they had always known and loved.

Their misgivings were unfortunately proven to be justified. Eventually Ben Butler beat Ellie to death in a violent rage. He was alone with her that day. Ellie had been left with an untreated shoulder fracture in the seven weeks leading up to her death. She sustained catastrophic head injuries eleven months after she was returned to her parents.

In June 2016 Ben Butler was convicted of her murder and jailed for life, with a minimum of 23 years. Ellie's mother perverted the course of justice by helping to cover up the murder. She lied about the little girl's time of death saying it was later than it actually was. For her part in it all, she was sentenced to 42 months in jail.

END NOTES

1. Claire Throssell on the Victoria Derbyshire show. https://www.youtube.com/watch?v=HjLjn4Iy4MU

2.https://www.instylemag.com.au/charlize-theron-family-mother-killed-her-father By Tina Burke n.d

3.https://www.theguardian.com/society/2018/apr/10/ellie-butler-unlawfully-killed-inquest-ben-butler 10th of April 2018 By Diane Taylor

4

Preparing And Planning To Leave

PSYCHING YOURSELF UP FOR THE TASK

If you ever find that you are now at the point where you decide that enough is enough and you want change, **a huge congratulations to you!** When the time comes that you come to the realization, that you deserve it and are worth more than what you have been putting up with, this is the beginning of a miracle! This in itself is a massive achievement and a giant leap in the right direction! It takes immense courage to think about it. It takes even more courage, to actually go through with whatever is necessary to make it happen. The way this thing ends depends largely on what you choose to do next. There is so much riding on this, but you do have what it takes to see it through! The proof is that in spite of all you have been through, you're still here.

Depending on your frame of mind you may find that once you have made the decision to leave, you feel relieved. On the other hand, you may find that once you have made such a decision, you literally go to pieces. It maybe that you are hit by the enormity of what you are about to do, with all its implications.

Whatever you feel at any given moment, is not necessarily a true reflection of the reality. Of course, emotions will undoubtedly be running high and this is totally understandable! The point is that you are taking the necessary steps to leave the abusive relationship, as a step to regain lost control of your life. This in itself will undoubtedly come with its challenges. The trick however is to get the pain and pressure you feel, working for you.

I won't lie to you. It will probably be one of the hardest decisions you ever have to make. It is however one that will set the tone for the rest of your life and will determine, how it all turns out in the end.

It is especially difficult when your emotions are all over the place. On top of that you may still feel as if in spite of everything, you still love your partner. This can be incredibly confusing for you to say the least.

Perhaps you are petrified by the very thought of going it alone, because you haven't done so for such a long time. Maybe you actually feel trapped, because you are financially dependent on your partner, and would not have a clue about how to go about changing that and moving forward.

In spite of all the many potential challenges however don't let anything stop you! The simple reason is that breaking out of the prison you have become accustomed to, will undoubtedly be one of the greatest moments of your life. The point is that if you so choose, this could be the beginning of the rest of your life!

One of the reasons why women often find it difficult to see the wood for the trees in terms of leaving the unhealthy relationship, is because they are plagued by the practical side of things.

Burning questions that you may ask yourself might include:

- If I leave where will I go?
- What sort of help is available to me?
- Where can I get appropriate advice?
- Who can help me move on with my life?
- Do I need to get myself a solicitor?
- If I need legal help how on earth will I pay for it?
- Do I have to speak to the police and make a statement?
- Do I have to go to court and see my ex- partner face to face?
- Will people actually believe me, considering how good he is at lying and pretending?
- How will I manage financially?
- How will contact between my ex-partner and my children work?
- Will they automatically live with me?

SECTION TWO

KEEPING SAFE AS YOU PLAN TO LEAVE

- Take the time you need to slowly pack your things. Try not to pack too many things all at once, so that there is no reason for your abuser to become suspicious of anything you are planning or doing. You can always get a police escort at a later date, to return to the property and collect the rest of your belongings. Initially just pack the most important things you will need during this emergency time, like your ID Documents, (passport, birth certificate, tenancy agreements, driving license, benefit letters, bank statements, bank cards, utility bills and proof of address. All these documents prove you are who you say you are and will be helpful to all the agencies that get involved in helping you. For instance, they will be used to register you at a refuge if you go to one, and to make a housing benefit claim, for that reason. Whenever a lady came to us at the refuge, it was so helpful if she managed to bring her paperwork with her. It was obviously understandable if she didn't, but it just made the process so much easier!

- It is a good idea to start keeping a journal, so that you can write about all the incidents that happen, as soon as they happen. That way, you will have a record of everything that has taken place to date. It will be easier to get the facts straight in your mind, while it is all fresh in your memory. If at a later stage you then decide you want to get legal help, it will be useful to help you remember, and as evidence of the terrible abuse you were subjected to. Remember to keep it in a safe place away from the prying eyes of your abuser.

- Keep a photo of your ex-partner so you know where it is when you need it. If you find yourself in the scenario where you ever need to report him to the police, the photo would give them a head start and show them exactly what he looks like. It will give them a good idea of who they are looking for, saving valuable time. This will really speed up the time it takes to find and deal with him, giving you peace of mind.

- If you feel threatened and as if you are in any danger at all at any time, do not hesitate to call the police! Don't worry about bothering them. It is their job to help and protect you. Besides it is far better for you to be safe than sorry.

- You will need clothes for you and your children, some of their favourite toys, toiletries, food, and any money you have, as well as any form of ID you have.

SECTION THREE

GOING INTO A REFUGE

WHAT IS A REFUGE?

Definition: A place that gives protection or shelter from danger, trouble, unhappiness (The Cambridge dictionary).

When it comes to answering the pressing questions you probably have regarding what to do, where to go, and how to go about it all, help is at hand! One alternative possibility is to take advantage of being able to go into a 'safe house,' also referred to as a refuge.

As the name suggests, basically it amounts to a form of short term emergency accommodation. A refuge is essentially a safe place where you live with other women and children who are also survivors of domestic violence, on a temporary basis. Here you can find respite from being pursued, harassed, and endangered every day of your precious life!

HOW LONG WILL I HAVE TO STAY
AT THE REFUGE?

The time scale of living at a refuge, varies from place to place, and from person to person. It will depend primarily on your own individual circumstances. You may be able to eventually return to your own property if and when safety measures are put in place. Alternatively, you may be blessed enough to start again by getting rehoused somewhere else, (in a different part of the country perhaps).

The refuge I worked at operated on an initial four-week license agreement basis. This meant that you would stay for four weeks, in the first instance. If it became necessary however, that time would be extended. There was no hard and fast rule about this. The point is, being at a refuge is only supposed to be short term emergency accommodation. It is however offered on a flexible basis at the particular refuge's discretion.

WHY GO INTO A REFUGE?

Yes, there is no doubt about it, moving into a refuge certainly is a huge step. Leaving an abusive relationship is probably one of the most traumatic times of your life, and to have made such a decision would not have been an easy one. It is a big deal to go along with it as your plan of action, and to follow it through.

Bearing this in mind, it is perhaps helpful to see the process as a new chapter of your life, with a new focus. Going into a refuge is the stepping stone to greater and better, although this will take time to manifest! It is most definitely different to living in your own home, so it will no doubt take getting used to and adjusting accordingly, to the idea as well as the reality of it.

HOW DO I GO ABOUT SECURING REFUGE SPACE?

Usually you can call a helpline number to refer yourself to get a space, or you can go through other agencies. Such agencies include the police, social services, probation services, youth offending team, homeless section of the council, medical staff, as well as voluntary organizations.

The refuge I worked at, offered a twenty-four, hour service. This meant that you could ring our help line number even in the middle of the night, if you needed emergency help. As long as we had the space you needed, and you fitted our criteria, the chances were, you would be accepted and eligible to secure yourself a space with us.

The point is that a refuge is meant to be a stop gap for you. Hopefully it will prove to be somewhere that provides you with breathing space to gather your thoughts, and consider your options in a safe, positive and warm environment.

WHY SHOULD I BE SECRETIVE ABOUT MY LEAVING PLANS?

If you do decide to go down this route and leave your home, it is absolutely imperative that you adopt and maintain, a high level of secrecy, regarding your plans to leave. Be very careful about who you choose to confide in. Do not trust everybody especially if you and the abuser have mutual friends.

Don't be too keen to share everything with family members either. Remember your ex-partner could and often will play dirty. In his relentless determination, he could wear them down, using the unscrupulous methods of either fear or manipulation, just to get to you. The way you decide to handle things, will narrow down the possibility of your violent ex, getting wind of what you are up to. In fact, the less people know the better, so there is less chance of a slip of the tongue.

WHY SHOULD I CHANGE MY PHONE NUMBER?

It is probably wise to change your phone number to avoid nuisance calls and being harassed. Ignore any phone calls from phone numbers that you don't recognize. It could be your ex or his (friends/family), just trying to catch you out! In this battle for your freedom, you will have to bear in mind that the enemy you face is ruthless and has absolutely no intention of playing fair! So be vigilant and stay alert!

WHAT IS A TYPICAL REFUGE LIKE?

There are different sized refuges. However, typically often there are rooms for single women, as well as family sized rooms suitable for women with children.

The refuge I worked at even had a room that had been specially adapted adequately for a disabled person. This meant that it was wheel chair friendly, had a walk-in shower, and a lift for easy access to other floors.

Some rooms had ensuite facilities. Others however had no bathroom and shower facilities, so the women assigned to these rooms all had to share the communal one also on the same floor. Each room was furnished and had a television and DVD player, to make things as comfortable as possible.

There was a shared kitchen operating on a self-catering basis. A woman was allocated a cupboard, freezer and fridge space to be able to store her food. There was also a shared lounge and dining room with a children's playroom attached. There was access to a laundry which was free to do any clothes washing. All that needed to be provided was washing powder.

There was a payphone in the corridor which allowed outgoing calls only. Next to it was a list of helpful numbers. Personal calls were not accepted on this phone unless it was an emergency.

Once a woman arrived at the refuge, she was shown around the building, so that she had the chance to become familiar with where everything was located. Staff would then explain the procedures at the refuge and how things would work during her stay. This would include the fire procedure, what to do if there is a fire, where all the fire exits are, (for emergency purposes). She was also shown where the staff office was in case she needed assistance from the staff at any time.

It would be explained how to contact staff if there was an emergency during out of hours periods, including where the staff flat was. This was necessary in case she needed help in the middle of the night.

Last but not least she was of course shown the room she was being assigned to. She was also shown all the facilities so that she would know exactly what was available to her, during her stay at the refuge.

Attached to the refuge was a nursery for any children aged between two and five. Mums were encouraged to allow their children to attend, as it was good for them and good for the children. Mum then had the opportunity for some much needed 'me time,' where she could have time and space to think.

The children had the opportunity to take part in activities that were designed to give them the chance to play and just be kids!

For older children there were after school clubs, and Saturday morning club. These were specifically tailored to the needs of the children from a domestically violent background. Through play, the activities provided an opportunity to address and deal with issues that would have inevitably arisen, because of the things they had been through and witnessed.

Apart from these clubs and activities, a woman was completely responsible for her children at all times. The refuge required them to supervise their children around the building as well as in the play area. They also had to send the children to school. A school welfare officer visited regularly to ensure all the children at the refuge were attending school during their stay.

To empower the women, we supported them to get involved in service user meetings, where they could get used to expressing themselves in a safe environment. They had the opportunity to discuss things with one another regarding the refuge, including any issues that had arisen, as well as any suggestions that they may have, about how to improve the facilities. This meeting also provided an opportunity to find out any information they needed.

We also encouraged them to organize any events they wanted to get involved in like cooking, movie nights, or trips. On the surface these appeared to be very simple things, however they went a long way towards giving them a sense of achievement and accomplishment. These were things they were choosing to do and participate in, without being violently forced to do so, as well as things they had been forbidden to do by their abuser!

We discouraged the ladies from lending one another things especially money, and clothes. Entering one another's rooms was also something not encouraged. The idea was that it scaled down on what could go wrong, like things going missing, or just not being returned. In-fact the women were instructed to lock their room doors whenever stepping out or at night.

WHAT PRACTICAL HELP CAN I EXPECT TO GET ON ARRIVAL?

At the refuge sometimes, toiletries and a few clothes were provided initially. There was also access to an emergency cupboard full of food. These things were donated by various people, over time. (These people were often from all walks of life). Some from nearby churches. Others were just ordinary people who had more than they needed, and therefore decided to share out of their plenty, with those who they knew were less fortunate than they were.

In this way the refuge was kept constantly supplied with the needed resources, to be able to cater for any woman that arrived with no food, or toiletries or money of her own. If she was forced to make her move and leave in a great hurry, it was often typical that a woman would arrive, with nothing more than the clothes on her back! Sometimes she had to make her great escape by seizing the opportunity as it presented itself. That was not always at the most convenient of times, but often was very much a 'now or never moment'!

Strategically, the refuge staff were usually female. This was obviously to help vulnerable women and children to get their bearings, relax, and settle as soon as possible, without feeling threatened by the presence of a man.

Soon after a woman's arrival at the refuge, once she had been allowed a little time to catch her breath, she was interviewed by the staff. This was done as sensitively and as soon as possible practically speaking, while things are still fresh in her mind. The purpose of this is to gather as much background and personal information on the woman as possible. This enables the refuge (and any other agencies involved), to be in a better and stronger position to understand where she's coming from. Only then are they equipped to keep her safe, as well as help and support her as much as she requires. This will apply during her stay at the refuge, but also when she initially leaves to go into her own property.

Part of getting to know the lady would mean understanding the different agencies involved with her, and assessing what help she is receiving, as opposed to what help she actually needs. This helps to build a picture of the background she is coming from, as well as the help she is likely to need from here onwards.

The interview questions a woman was frequently asked would include details such as:

- What was her full name including any nicknames?
- What was her date of birth and did she have a birth certificate (which would be photocopied)?
- If she had children, their names and dates of birth (birth certificates also photocopied)
- Who was her next of kin?
- What was the number of the mobile phone she was using (so we could contact her safely if necessary)?
- What was her national insurance number?
- Which agency referred her to the refuge?
- What was the address of the property she was fleeing and how long had she lived there?
- Was the property rented or joint owned with ex-partner?
- What was the name, address and phone number of her usual GP?
- Was she working and where was her job?
- Was she on any benefit and which ones?
- What was her ethnic origin, and did she have any cultural needs and preferences?
- What was her legal status in the country?
- Did she have proof of ID such as a passport or immigration letters?
- Who was she at risk from (what is the name/address of the person/people she is fleeing from?

Obviously, every women and child that came to the refuge was unique and different, so some needed more support, and some needed less. The support each lady received was tailor made to suit each need, so the service we offered included adapting to whatever she needed. After-all each woman is unique with individual challenges. We actively assisted each one to develop practical skills, increase their independence, and self-confidence. Obviously, this is a process and a journey, that takes time.

On arrival at the refuge you will be allocated a key worker. Now obviously all the staff are available and on hand to help and assist you in any way that they can, with whatever you feel you need. Your key worker however is the one who will work very closely with you. She will support and assist you on your own particular unique journey, of trying to figure out what comes next, and what direction it would be best for you to take. She will help you to literally catch your breath. The ultimate aim here will undoubtedly be to work out a strategy to improve the quality of your life, and assist you to exercise your newly found gifts, of freedom and choice! You will also be able to express what you feel you need and want, in terms of support from the refuge service.

Your key worker will also carry out informative support sessions with you. During these times there will be many opportunities, to ask relevant questions and receive appropriate information. It is a chance to understand what sort of help you can expect to receive. At the end of each session, you will have completed support plans that can be built upon as your needs are established and change. This is important to ensure, that all your unique and particular needs are being catered for, once they are identified. Together you will look at housing, finances, budgeting, daily living skills, leisure and the social side of life. This is your opportunity to take back control of your life!

Hopefully then she can assist you to ensure that steps can be taken to meet those needs, and to formulate plans for you to be able to move forward. She will assist you to make phone calls, to arrange appointments, and to find out further information.

Hopefully after each session you will feel empowered and more confident! Every decision you make from this point on can be an informed decision. During the time between each support session you have with your key worker, you will both work together to complete any outstanding action needed, to be reviewed at subsequent sessions. The overall outcome of these support sessions is that you will be assisted to achieve your personal aims and goals. It is imperative that in time with the right help, you come to believe that indeed tomorrow can be a new and brighter day! Before long, you will be ready to face the world and move on to independent living.

The sessions will include sorting out your income including your work situation if you have a job, or your benefits if you are not working. You will receive help to make a new claim of which ever benefit you are entitled to. This will most likely include housing benefit, (to cover the rent for your stay at the refuge). Someone has to pay for your stay, so the benefit claim covers you so that you don't become liable to pay the full amount, which would work out to be very expensive.

You will also have to pay a minimal service charge, for being at the refuge which covers your electricity, water, heating, television license bills. Then you will be assisted and educated on how exactly to budget and manage your money.

You will need to inform the appropriate people, including your bank, current benefit office, children's school, of your change of address, so they will know where to send any current correspondence. You will also need to inform (whoever you usually pay your property utility bills to). It is important to give them updated information, so that they have the date when you actually left your previous property. You also want to ensure that they stop charging you, so that no-one will be able to run up the bills in your name!

It is also important and helpful to obtain temporary registration with the local general practitioner (GP) and medical centre, in case you fall ill during your time at the refuge.

You will be given information regarding local solicitors to help you through the legal stuff. (The refuge actually had particular solicitors they worked closely with and referred most of our women to). They had a lot of experience with domestic violence issues, and so were able to help, minimizing the trauma of having to go down the legal route.

You may find you need help and advice from social services, health visitors or just help with access to schools for your children. You will be sign posted to whichever services you need.

You will be supported to be able to address any understandable but inappropriate behaviour that you find yourself exhibiting. This will be by signposting you to the relevant agencies, for instance if you need help with anger management, or addiction and substance abuse. To be able to kick start any of the above help, your key worker will make a note on your support plan, of all the actions that need to be taken to get your life back on track.

You will be supported to develop effective relations with relevant outside agencies, that will focus on your welfare and that of your children. The aim here is to ensure that your needs are being met.

At the refuge we encouraged the women to maintain any networks they already had, including seeing family members, being part of a social community, as well as cultural and leisure activities. The idea was to get them socializing again, (after being isolated for so long). It may be quite a bit of a process to get them used to being with people again.

The refuge also ran a six-week course for the women. It was aimed at raising awareness about domestic violence and all it entails. The idea was that the more a woman understands about what she has been through, the better equipped she will be to keep herself safe in the future. For a woman who has been a victim of domestic violence, there is so much to unlearn before she can even begin to learn a new way of thinking. This is especially true if she has suffered in this way for years. She would have become accustomed to believing lies. This can be to such an extent, that it becomes almost impossible to distinguish the difference between what is true and what is not.

This works in the same way as detoxification. When you are addicted to something, or someone, it takes time to go cold turkey, let go, and move on with a new and different mindset. As bad and difficult as things get within an abusive relationship, it becomes familiar and what you get used to. It takes a steely determination to break free, from the thinking that goes hand in hand with being a victim of domestic violence. It takes even more to feel it is a battle worth fighting, and one that you feel you even have the energy, strength or desire to even want to.

Working at the refuge, unfortunately I saw many women either return to the abusive relationship they had left or enter into a new one that was equally abusive or worse. This is proof that the effects of domestic violence are far reaching, and so much more than just a physical thing. Obviously yes it does take an abuser, but it also takes the victim enabling the situation, by being caught up in completely wrong and destructive thinking.

The course helps with this process of a renewed way of thinking. Participating in it teaches what domestic violence is on a basic level, as well as giving much needed tips, regarding the most empowering way to move forward. The fact is, it takes the implementation of a completely new way of thinking for your life to change in the right way. The course attempts to help with that, by giving information that a woman was perhaps previously unfamiliar with. This can range from her rights, to what is unacceptable in a relationship, as well as when a relationship is healthy as well as unhealthy.

It is vital that your transition period strengthens your hope and belief, that you no longer have to feel as if you have to deal with things on your own. Making you feel welcome while putting you at ease, should be the objective of the refuge staff and serve as a breath of fresh air for you.

Admittedly you may struggle initially with the whole refuge setup. It may be the first time in a long time that you feel as if anyone cares about you, and is actually listening to you, for a change. Understandably that in itself will take some serious getting used to, as it will feel completely unfamiliar and even alien to you.

Living in a refuge is obviously not the same as being in the comfort of your own home. It may not be easy to get used to communal living. As such there will be a lack of privacy as you will have to share in a way you are not used to. You may find it noisy with other families around. There may be personality clashes between you and other women living there. This is however taken into account when a refuge is setup. Bearing this in mind they are significantly adapted to be as comfortable as possible, as well as fit for purpose, away from home.

WHAT ARE SOME OF THE ADVANTAGES OF GOING INTO A REFUGE?

One of the many advantages of going into a refuge is that you will be adequately supported. As result all sorts of information which was previously hidden from you, will suddenly become totally available. Your experience at the refuge, will hopefully enable you to become an empowered woman equipped to deal with life.

You will be taught safety planning in every sense of the word. The idea is so that you learn how to keep yourself safe from harm...especially in light of the domestically violent experience you have managed to come through and survive.

There is no getting away from it...What you have come through is absolutely horrendous. As you have however lived to tell the tale, having the opportunity to physically remove yourself, is an essential step in the right direction.

If you need help with sorting out your choices regarding

housing, your keyworker can help you. She can help you to apply for a new tenancy in the area you choose. She can book you an appointment with a housing officer to further assist you if necessary.

WHY SHOULD I NOT RETURN TO MY RISK AREA?

It is wise to avoid returning to the location area where you found yourself at risk. It would not be in your best interest or helpful, obviously for you to be spotted by 'the enemy' in the form of your ex, his family or friends. Moving out of the area, gives you the maximum opportunity to start again, and enjoy the blessing of freedom. This is your right and the choice you should be able to make.

The last thing that you want, is a situation where he is once again able to harass and threaten you. You do not want to find yourself back in a position where you are helpless, vulnerable, and where your safety is completely at risk.

Once you leave the property you once called home and are safely at the refuge, if you do receive any threats from your ex-partner, it is still a very good idea to report them to the police. If you receive them as texts, keep them as evidence for if you ever decide to take things to court.

You will also be sign posted to all the right agencies depending on whatever your needs are. This is a true example where knowledge truly is power. That power previously stolen from you, is now being offered back to you and is within reach.

WHY IS THE LOCATION AND ADDRESS OF THE REFUGE KEPT SECRET?

The location and address of a refuge is kept secret and totally confidential. This is obviously so that it cannot be easily located and found by the wrong person. There are many refuges throughout the United Kingdom so that you will have the opportunity to move completely away from wherever you usually live. The point is that you will be able to move out of the area, and therefore out of reach of your abusive partner. The important decisions you need to be able to make, and the conclusions you need to come to, need to be done free from the pressures of an abusive environment.

WILL THE REFUGE BE ABLE TO CATER FOR MY PARTICULAR ETHNIC BACKGROUND?

The refuge I worked at catered for the basic needs of women from various ethnic backgrounds including Asian, Polish, Caribbean, African etc.

Alternatively, there are refuges that cater for specific ethnic groups. This is vitally important for some women. These types of refuges exist, because they recognize that it really helps to make an already challenging and drastic change that little bit easier, for the women involved. Imagine how difficult it would be if you were Asian or polish, and you had the added challenge of not being able to speak very much English. This is unfortunately the reality of many women. This is the reason why these types of refuges help to make an already difficult situation, slightly more manageable, than if these women had no choice but to go to a general refuge, where they felt isolated and alienated.

Immigration may be an issue. This applies especially if your status in a country like the United Kingdom is unclear. Things could get even more complicated if your financial security, has been dependent on the husband you are trying to flee from. However regardless of your circumstances, the police, and the law have a duty to help you whenever you need it.

If it is proven that you have no right in the United Kingdom, then things could get very challenging. Your case will be referred to, as having no recourse to public funds. You unfortunately will be unable to claim any benefits initially.

As I explained earlier, some refuges run a twenty-four hour service. This means that you can ring up any hour of the day to receive advice, or to be referred and receive temporary accommodation elsewhere. Other refuges only operate on a nine to five basis. The point is that you have choice and can choose not to stay in a domestically violent environment!

Whenever a woman or family left the refuge, it was our policy to do a safe and well check. This entailed phoning her a week after she left. The idea was to check that all was alright with her, as well as whether or not she needed anything. She also had the option of a home visit from a member of staff from the refuge. This would continue for as long as she felt she needed the support.

HELPFUL AGENCIES TO CONTACT

- **NATIONAL REFUGES:** These are safe houses all across the country that offer emergency accommodation, (a safe place to stay and therefore an opportunity to leave the domestically violent environment behind).

- **CALDMORE HOUSING WOMEN'S REFUGE:** This is a refuge for vulnerable women and children. It is a safe place for them to stay. Phone: 01922 476574

- **CHANGING PATHWAYS:**
  Contact: www.changingpathways.org/refuge
  Phone: 01268 729707
  Email: referrals@changingpathways.org

- **BIRMINGHAM AND SOLIHULL WOMEN'S AID:**
  Phone: 0808 8000028
  Email: info@bswaid.org

- **BLACK COUNTRY WOMEN'S AID:**
  Email: info@blackcountrywomensaid.co.uk
  Phone:01384455411

- **BRISTOL WOMEN'S AID:**
  Phone: 0808 2000247
  Email: helpline@womensaid.org.uk

- **CHESHIRE WITHOUT ABUSE:**
  This organization offers access to crisis accommodation, support, advice and recovery programmes.
  Phone: 01270 250390
  https://www.cheshirewithoutabuse.org.uk/contact

- **COVENTRY HAVEN WOMEN'S AID:**
  Phone: 0808 2000 247. (out of hours)
  Email: info@coventryhaven.co.uk

- **DERBY WOMEN'S CENTRE:**
  Phone: 01332 341633
  Email: elainer@derbywomenscentre.co.uk (outside of centre hours)

- **GLASGOW WOMEN'S AID:**
  Phone: 0141 5532022
  http://www.glasgowwomensaid.org.uk/contact-us.html

- **HESTIA:**
  This is a charity based in London that provide refuge from domestic violence. They provide practical and emotional support for vulnerable traumatised women and children.
  Phone: 020 7378 3102
  Email: Info@hestia.org
  https://www.hestia.org/brightsky

- **HARBOUR MIDDLESBOROUGH:**
  Phone: 01642 861788 (24hr) or 01642 231094
  Email: info@myharbour.org.uk
  Website: www.myharbour.org.uk

- **KENT (OASIS WOMEN'S REFUGE):**
  Phone: 01843269400
  Email: enquiries@oasisdaservice.org

- **LEEDS WOMEN'S AID:**
  administration@leedswomensaid.org.uk
  Phone: 0113 2460401

- **LOWESTOFT/ GREAT YAMOUTH**
  (LIBERTY PROJECT):
  Phone: 0845 4671420 or 0808 2000247 (24hr)

- **MANCHESTER WOMEN'S AID:**
  Phone: 0161 6367525 or 080820000247 (24hr)
  Email: referrals@manchesterwomensaid.org

- **NATIONAL WOMEN'S AID:**
  Phone: 0808 2000247
  Email: helpline@womensaid.org.uk

- **NOTTINGHAMSHIRE WOMEN'S AID:**
  Contact: enquires@nottswa.org
  Phone: 0808 0800 0340
  01909 533610

- **NORTH KIRKLEES WOMEN'S REFUGE:**
  Phone: 01924 465238
  Email: hello@connecthousing.org.uk

- **NUNEATON AND BEDWORTH WOMEN'S AID:**
  0800 408 1552
  Email: DVSW@refuge.org.uk

- **PANAHGHAR ASIAN WOMEN'S REFUGE:**
  This is a charity based in Coventry catering for primarily Asian women.
  Contact: www.safehouse.org.uk
  Phone: 02476 228952

- **POLISH DOMESTIC VIOLENCE HELPLINE:**
  01270 260106

- **ROSHNI REFUGE:**
  For Asian women
  Phone: 0870 7070098
  Email: admin@roshnibirmingham.org.uk

- **SANDWELL WOMEN'S AID:**
  Phone: 0121 5530090

- **SOLACE WOMEN'S AID: (LONDON)**
  Phone: 0808 8025565
  advice@solacewomensaid.org

- **STAFFORDSHIRE WOMEN'S AID:**
  Phone: 0300 330 5959

- **THE HAVEN: (WOLVERHAMPTON)**
  Phone: 01902 904677 or 0800 0194400 (24hrs)
  Email: info@havenrefuge.org.uk

- **THE PATHWAY PROJECT (THE HOPE CENTRE):**
  This organization was started by a lady who is a survivor of domestic violence. They offer accommodation in safe houses for people who need some where to stay. They also offer a service for men who are also victims, offering support, advice and counselling.
  Helpline Email – Talktoeve.pathway@virgin.net
  24-hr helpline – 01543 676 800

OTHER AGENCIES (What they do and provide)

- **CAP MONEY COURSE:** This is a course that is run to help people to learn how to manage and handle their money. It is a completely free course which you can do in a relaxed and fun environment.
  Phone: 01274 760720
  CAP New Client Enquiries: 0800 328 0006
  Contact: info@capmoneycourse.org

- **CHILD FIRST:**

On the 20th of January 2016, there was a report on the BBC Victoria Derbyshire programme. The report was done as too many children's lives were being put at risk by family courts decisions. The fact is vulnerable children were being forced to continually have contact with abusive parents.

Women's aid therefore launched a new campaign as a result, as something needed to be done urgently. The goal of this campaign is to put children's safety back at the heart and centre of family court decisions. This is after all where it has always belonged. The vital issue of children's safety has unfortunately not always been where it should be. So many cases have highlighted this where sadly there has been tragic loss of life, precious children gone, because the system has failed them! All were killed by domestic violence perpetrators deliberately!

Between the years of 2005 and 2015 there have been nineteen recorded homicides. Every single one of them happened because contact between the children and their violent parent was agreed, arranged and in fact went ahead. In hindsight, it turned out to be a grave mistake, totally unwise and completely unsafe. The harsh reality is that these deaths should never have happened! They could and should have been avoided!

The campaign now focuses on doing a thorough investigation, to ascertain whether or not there has been any domestic violence in the history of each case. The campaign places special emphasis on the safety and welfare of the victims, (children and their mothers), as their priority and at the heart of things.

phone: (203) 538-5222
Email: info@childfirst.org

- **CHILDHOOD DOMESTIC VIOLENCE ASSOCIATION:**
This is an organization that was founded by Brian F
Martin in 2007. He founded it because he experienced
domestic violence as a child. This made him therefore
determined to help other people going through the
same thing. The organization now focuses on helping
to increase awareness, and provides practical tools to
help and empower children, who have been victims. It
enables them to learn and develop the skills to be able to
move forward in their lives.
Contact: info@cdv.org

- **CHILDLINE:**
This is an organization that was set up to help children
with whatever challenging issues they may find
themselves dealing with. It aims to let them know they
are not alone in their struggle.
Contact: www.childline.org.uk
Phone: 0800 1111

- **CLAIMING MAINTENANCE SAFELY:**
This is an agency that deals with sorting out the paying and
receiving of child maintenance for a child.
https://www.gingerbread.org.uk/information/child-
maintenance/domestic-abuse-and-child-maintenance
Phone: 0207 428 5400

- **EATING DISORDERS HELP: PRIORY GROUP**
  This organization deals with eating disorders as well as different types of addictions, including alcohol, drugs, etc
  Contact: www.priorygroup.com
  Phone: 0800 6911387

- **FEMALE GENITAL MUTILATION:**
  There is help for girls and women who are at risk or have already been affected by this.
  Contact: fgmhelp@nspcc.org.uk
  FGM Helpline: 0800 0283550

- **FORCED MARRIAGE HELP:**
  Phone: 0800 5999247
  Contact: www.karmanirvana.org.uk/

- **FCO (Forced Marriage Unit)**
  Phone:0207 0080151 or 00442070080151 if calling for help from abroad.

- **GINGERBREAD HELPLINE:**
  This is a charity for single parents, offering practical help, support and advice, covering various topics and challenges.
  Contact: www.gingerbread.org.uk
  Phone: 0808 8020925

- **HEALTH CARE PROFESSIONALS:** These include anyone who is a midwife, doctor, dentist, health visitor. Any of these people would be involved in helping to keep you healthy. When you are going to see one of them at an appointment, this may be your moment and the only chance you get to sound the alarm and ask for their help. These professionals are on the frontline, and therefore have a good opportunity to identify you, if you are suffering from domestic violence, as they may be able to recognise the signs. They often develop and establish support networks, and therefore may be in the perfect position to be able to signpost you in the right direction. This could get you the help you need and present the opportunity for you to finally have contact with the 'outside world,' and break free from your abuser and the prison he has forced you to live in!

- **MODERN SLAVERY HELPLINE:**
  Phone: 0800 0121700
  www.modernslaveryhelpline.org/report

- **IKWRO:**
  This is an organization that was originally founded for Iranian and Kurdish women to uphold their rights. They provide culturally specific support, for middle Eastern women who have survived honour-based violence.
  Contact: 0207 9206460
  http://ikwro.org.uk/contact-us/

- **KARMA NIRVANA:** This is a charity that helps to prevent forced marriage and honour-based abuse. They provide training, as well as practical and emotional support.

Phone: 0800 5999247 or 01138870281
Mob: 07929050163
Email: a.manota@karmanirvana.org.uk
www.karmanirvana.org.uk

- **LANGUAGE INTERPRETERS:**
The services of language interpreters are vital in many cases for some women. It makes it possible for them to be able to obtain help and access to the services they need, particularly when they are from a completely different country, and challenged by the language barrier.

Often the women that came to the refuge did not speak English as their first language. They were already completely traumatised by their experiences. On top of that they also had the added challenge of the language barrier. This meant they could not communicate effectively and make themselves understood. This compounded the difficulty and pressure they felt, because communicating with them was a major problem. They felt even more frightened, and as if the combination of everything was too much to bear.

The only way to successfully assist them therefore was to call on the help and expertise of an interpreter. The service was incredibly helpful to these women, so that they could have conversations, as well as things explained to them in a language they could understand. As a support worker, it was part of my job to arrange for an interpreter to assist them if one was needed.

- **NATIONAL CENTRE FOR DOMESTIC VIOLENCE:**
  They are an organization that give legal advice and
  provide fast emergency legal help.
  Phone: 0800 9702070
  Website: www.ncdv.org.uk

- **NATIONAL EXPRESS: (Coach and bus travel)**
  Phone: 0871 7818181

- **NATIONAL SOCIETY FOR THE PREVENTION OF
  CRUELTY TO CHILDREN (NSPCC):**
  This organization is also known as child line. Essentially,
  they focus on fighting for childhood, by preventing
  abuse which forces children to grow up too quickly.
  Children can ring the helpline to get information or to
  speak to a counsellor, call: 0800 1111 (For children and
  young people) 0808 800 5000 (For adults concerned
  about a child)

- **NATIONAL RAIL ENQUIRIES:**
  Contact Centre number: 03457 484 950
  Customer Relations number: 08000 223 720

- **NETWORK FOR SURVIVING STALKING:**
  National stalking helpline: 08088020300
  Contact: www.stalkinghelpline.org
  Email: advice@stalkinghelpline.org

- **NO PANIC:**
  This organization help and give advice to people who suffer from panic attacks, anxiety, phobias, and obsessive, compulsive disorders. Contact: www.nopanic.org.uk
  Phone: 0844 9674848

- **PLAY THERAPY UK:**
  This is an organization that uses play and creative arts to help children in a therapeutic way. Here the children are encouraged to express themselves and share what's on their minds, but they are not obliged to use words. The aim is to help the child emotionally, while sensitively addressing any behavioural issues they may have, at the same time. This encourages the child to heal and equips them to develop coping strategies to be able to move forward, and be healthy in life, putting behind them the trauma they have been through.
  Contact: 01825 761143

- **POLICE:**
  The police provide practical help in a crisis emergency situation. Essentially, they deal with crime and enforce the law. In an emergency phone: 999 or non-emergency call 101 (West Midlands Police)

In an emergency, a woman experiencing domestic violence is well within her rights to call the police for help. If she finds herself being subjected to violent behaviour from her partner, it is wise to get the police involved and to accept their intervention, rather than risk being harmed by an abusive situation.

For this reason, often in this sort of unfortunate scenario, they are the first ones on the scene, and as a result they have an incredibly vital role to play. It is important for them to ensure that everyone involved, especially (you and your children are kept safe as a priority)! It is their job to make sure that all harm to anyone is kept to a minimum, and therefore any source of violence is to be removed by them as quickly as possible.

Depending on what exactly has happened, medical help and assistance may be needed. In that case, they will also call an ambulance for you, to make sure you are taken care of as soon as possible. It may become necessary to physically remove and arrest the abuser, because his presence poses a very real possible threat to you.

Another job the police can also do is provide you with a 'police escort.' Sometimes women have no choice but to leave their home in a tremendous hurry with just the clothes on their back. In these cases, they are within their rights to call the police, to escort them back to the property that they are fleeing from. The idea is so that she can collect any of her remaining belongings safely, and with the protection of the police. That way if there are any problems it is not up to her, but up to the police to deal with and sort out.

At some point in the very near future, it is the responsibility of the police to find out exactly what happened between you and your abusive partner, and then to take a statement from you. During this process, they should make sure they give you the opportunity to give your side of the story, putting you at ease. They should do all they can to remove every feeling of intimidation, you might be feeling. As they deal with you, it is imperative that they really do bear in mind the trauma you have already experienced. They should adopt the most sensitive manner possible, to gather the necessary information from you.

There have been times unfortunately, when women have been dealt with by police officers who have come across (to them) as uncaring and unsupportive. These women have courageously explained to the police officers what has taken place on the home front. They have often done so, only to be left feeling as if the police did not believe their story. This has had terrible consequences including a complete failure to carry out adequate risk assessments, regarding the victims.

In other cases, at times these vulnerable women have been dealt with by police officers who are not specialized in, the area of domestic violence. This has of course meant that the officers are not properly equipped or experienced enough, to put these women at ease. They are often quite clueless when it comes to dealing with them in the best way possible. It is then so difficult to get a conclusion that is helpful, fruitful, productive, and satisfactory for the women involved.

The unfortunate reality is that the number of women, that are being subjected to the crime of domestic violence is simply astronomical, and sadly growing. The truth therefore is that the police force and other relevant agencies, can never boast of having too much training when it comes to adequately dealing with them!

Training for police officers at the most basic level, is the least that should be expected on every force. It really should not matter which part of the country the police officers are based. This should be the mandatory and the absolute standard nationwide! There should also be ongoing renewed training available. This is so that, as the issues that affect victims of domestic violence come to light and evolve, the police involved will be able to provide the necessary help and support, needed on any level at the most crucial moments.

As of the 21st of September 2015, it was highlighted in the news that police forces were being given a checklist. The idea behind this is for them to become familiar with spotting the signs of domestic violence. From now on therefore, they will receive more training and guidance. The hope is that the police force, will become much more efficient and effective, at the whole necessary business of having to deal with vulnerable women. As this drastically improves, perhaps then these women will be more willing to be open and co-operate better with the police. This is vitally important, especially when you consider that the police are often the initial point of contact a woman has with the outside world. (First on the scene so to speak).

The special training will include giving the police force important guidelines, that will help them do much better in this area. They will be taught and encouraged to focus on the evidence of the case, and go by that, rather than just by the verbal testimony of the victim involved. The reason for this is that the victim could quite possibly have been influenced, and their testimony contaminated by the trauma they have been through! To be honest the police have got their work cut out, and the seriousness of their role can easily be seen, when it comes to victims of domestic violence. Choosing to believe a woman's story or not, is so crucial when you consider that it can literally come down to it being a question of life or death! It really is that cut and dry!

When I worked at the refuge, I came into contact, with countless women who were petrified of dealing with the police. Some in fact flatly refused to report the crime of domestic violence that they had suffered. The reason was always that they did not feel they would be taken seriously but would instead, be blamed for the turn of events.

Granted sometimes it is very difficult, for the police to understand mentally where the victims are coming from. This will however never be a good enough excuse to deal with them shabbily. In any interaction, victims should never be left feeling intimidated, or as if they are just wasting everyone's time.

As of the 15th of December 2015, in the news apparently the police force in England and Wales admitted that they are close to being 'overwhelmed,' because they have seen such a significant increase in domestic violence!

At the same time, there is still a great need as (we have already established), for the police to completely re-access the way they do things with regard, to subject of domestic violence. There must be a complete change in the way they deal with the whole subject, and subsequently with the way they handle vulnerable women. The tendency to stereotype and prejudge on all levels, needs to stop and become a thing of the past!

This is so vital as we have already established, because women have been discouraged from bothering to co-operate with the police. They have found it a pointless, frustrating exercise. Quite often they find it very difficult to see the point, of wasting their energy to come forward in the first place to report the crime, make a statement, or follow through with pressing charges. In some cases, having to deal with the police, has been such an unpleasant experience, that it has in fact added to the trauma they have already experienced!

- **WITNESS PROTECTION SYSTEM:**
  The police can help people to enter into the witness protection system, when a victim finds their life is under severe threat. This scenario could arise when the police believe that they can no longer offer adequate protection for them. The victim is then left with no choice but to say goodbye to all they know, including their family, friends, and neighbourhood. They have to move to another part of the country, where nobody knows them to give them the chance to start life again, and therefore a new identity will be created for them. This is obviously a life changing situation and therefore one which cannot be taken lightly.
  Phone: In an emergency call 999
  For non-emergency call 101
  West Midlands Police: 0345 1135000

If the police attend a domestic violence incident at your home address, they will often write to you shortly afterwards confirming that it was established that you were the victim, and they will reassure you that they are dedicated to the safety of you and your children, as you work with them to prevent any further incidents. They will also inform you of other agencies that can help with your safety planning and are available to assist you. They will give you the opportunity to speak to one of their domestic abuse officers in confidence if you feel it will be of benefit to you. They will also write to the person who abused you, to inform them that they will act whenever there is an incident, actively implementing any necessary safety measures.

- **RAPE CRISIS ENGLAND AND WALES:**
  https://rapecrisis.org.uk/contact-us/
  Email: rcewinfo@rapecrisis.org.uk

- **RELATE:**
  This organization offers support to people who are experiencing difficulty in their relationships.
  Contact: www.relate.org.uk/relationship
  Phone: 0300 1001234

- **RESPECT:**
  This organization help perpetrators of domestic violence by working with violent offenders, who have decided they want to change and accept that they need help to stop being abusive. They are taught how to change their own behaviour by taking full responsibility for their actions. This enables them to be able to make different choices, instead of blaming everything and everyone else. Only then will he be able to work hard and apply what he has learned, to make sure he stops being abusive.
  Respect Phoneline on freephone 0808 802 4040
  Email info@respect.uk.net

- **RIGHTS OF WOMEN LEGAL ADVICE LINE:**
  They offer legal advice for people suffering from

domestic violence. They also specialize in family law as well as immigration issues.
Contact: www.rightsofwomen.org.uk
Phone: 020 7251 8887 Criminal law
020 7251 6577 Family law
020 7490 7689 Immigration and asylum
Email: info@row.org.uk

- **SAYA:**
This organization provides a multilingual help line where woman can obtain support, advice and information if they are victims of domestic violence and English is not their first language.
Help line: 0800 389 6990

- **SILENCE HIDES VIOLENCE:**
Brook Beaton launched an anti-abuse campaign after being attacked by her boyfriend. She posted photos of herself on social media getting an incredible response as it went viral. She used her situation to raise awareness about Domestic violence.

- **SOCIAL SERVICES:**
Typically, they become involved with a family to offer help and support, especially when they are struggling and going through a difficult and challenging time. One of their main priorities is to safeguard the vulnerable, including children.

A social worker is assigned to the family to help them work through any problems, that may have arisen as a result of domestic violence that they have had to live with. This is particularly relevant when there is evidence that the family are victims because they are been threatened by and subjected to domestic violence.

As soon as possible, there is usually an initial assessment to ascertain what sort of help is needed. It may become necessary for the child's safety, for it to be placed in temporary foster care, preferably with all parties including (social services and the parent) in agreement with this course of action. The process will all be arranged and carried out through social services.

If there is an emergency situation that calls for the police to get involved because there is a court order in place, which requires their presence, then social services would automatically be involved as they would be responsible for 'taking the child into care.'

Social services are also responsible for arranging a 'child protection conference.' This usually involves getting together all the different agencies involved in the child's life. The parties will set out to establish what all the concerns are, as well as the best way to protect the child. This is the priority and first concern of everyone involved.

They will write to you to confirm the details of the initial Child Protection Conference which will be arranged as a consequence of any Child Protection concerns that have been highlighted regarding your child. It is very important that you attend a Child Protection Conference which is a meeting in which the family and professionals (including social services, and the police), concerned with your child, are provided with an opportunity to exchange information and make plans for the future. They will explain where the meeting is to be held so you know where to attend. You will also be given the opportunity to meet with social services before hand to read the report, and to go through the process of the meeting so you know exactly what to expect.

A protection plan for the child will be drawn up and agreed, so that all parties are on the same page and can decide together how best to move forward, with the child's welfare at the forefront.

- ◆ **TAX CREDIT OFFICE:**
  Contact: www.inlandrevenue.gov.uk/taxcredits
  Phone:0845 300 3900

- ◆ **THE FREEDOM PROGRAMME:**
  This is a domestic violence programme which was created by a lady called Pat Craven. The course usually runs for twelve weeks and was developed primarily to educate women as victims, and men as perpretrators. Its aim is to teach people, the value of understanding the way that their attitudes have a major impact on their relationships, and consequently how they turn out in the end. Ofcourse coming out of a domestically violent relationship situation is crucial, but equally so is receiving the education necessary to bring about lasting change to all the parties involved!
  Contact: www.freedomprogramme.co.uk
  24 hr freedom programme helpline: 01942 262270

- **THE HIDEOUT:**
  This is a website that has been created by women's aid, specifically for children and young people. It was created as a way of giving them the opportunity to get access to information that can help them. Domestic violence is such a complex issue even for adults. Young people therefore need to have it explained in a way they can understand, to enable them to be able to recognise and understand what has been incredibly traumatic for them. They can then hopefully work out what they can do, and who they can contact to get the appropriate help that they need.
  Contact: www.thehideout.org.uk
  Phone: NSPCC 0800 056 0566

- **THE SAMARITANS:**
  The main thing the Samaritans offer is a confidential, listening ear. They operate on a twenty-four hour basis, and people can call and talk about anything at all, that bothers them. They don't necessarily have to be suicidal. The staff will listen to them without being judgmental.
  Contact: http://www.samaritans.org
  Help line: 0845 7909090

- **THE SNOW DROP PROJECT:**
  This is a charity that specializes in dealing with people who have been victims of modern slavery and human trafficking. It was founded to provide support, (temporary and long term to people who have been traumatized in this way). They provide a good

understanding of the subject as well as practical help and support. For more information please contact them directly.

Tel: 0333 880 5008

Email: info@snowdropproject.co.uk

- ◆ **TRIDENT REACH MEN'S DOMESTIC VIOLENCE SERVICE BIRMINGHAM:**
  This organization provides a service that caters for men who are victims of domestic
  violence. They offer emotional and practical support so that these men are able to get their lives back on track after the trauma they have been through.
  Contact: Birmingham: https://tridentreach.org.uk/reach/birmingham/domestic-abuse-support-services
  South Derbyshire: https://tridentreach.org.uk/reach/derbyshire/domestic-abuse-support-service
  Phone: 0121 226 5800

- ◆ **VICTIM SUPPORT:**
  This charity helps people who have been victims of a crime, providing them with a listening ear and practical support. This may include escorting you to the police station if you need to report a crime, as well as going to court with you to give evidence. They also signpost you to other relevant agencies. They can help you understand how things work regarding court, especially if you are unfamiliar with the process. They can arrange for you to get the opportunity to have a look around court before you are due to go on the day of the case, so that you

know what to expect. Hopefully this will help make the experience less intimidating, and you would be less likely to have to deal with any unexpected surprises. They can also help you to fill out expense forms. They support you in any way that will help to make life easier for you.Contact: https://www.victimsupport.org.uk/ Phone: 0808 1689111

- **VISUAL EVIDENCE FOR VICTIMS (VEV):**
  This organization take photographs, specifically to record the evidence of the domestic violence you have suffered as well as any other crimes that have been committed against you. This is an opportunity to photograph any injuries you suffered, as well as photos of damage done to your property. As pictures are so good at telling the story perfectly, if you are taking the case to court the photos can be used as legal evidence to support your case, as they will speak volumes about what has really been taking place behind closed doors.

- **WOMEN'S AID:**
  This is one of the biggest and most well- known, organizations that works hard to help women and children who have experienced domestic violence. They provide practical help, support and advice. They also provide access to language line for women who need an Interpreter, because English is not their first language. 24 hour National domestic violence helpline 08082000247

- **AVON 'THE COMPANY FOR WOMEN':**
  Avon is the company for women that sells beauty products. It supports women's causes globally including end violence against women. It raises funds for such purposes. They also launched the 'Avon speak out against domestic violence program,' which tries to bring awareness, educate, develop and facilitate prevention. They do this by encouraging conversation and using their voice to highlight the many aspects of domestic violence, and what can be done to bring an end to it wherever it is found operating against women.
  Contact: https://www.avonworldwide.com supporting-women/violence-against-women-and-girls

WHO CAN MAKE A REFERRAL FOR CARE AND SUPPORT FOR VULNERABLE VICTIMS OF DOMESTIC VIOLENCE?

1. Social services

2. Probation service

3. Youth offending team

4. Police

5. Council (Homeless section)

6. Housing Association

7. Private Landlord

8. Doctors (GP)

9. Hospital

10. CPN (Community Psychiatric Nurse)

11. Relative/friend

12. Self-referral

13. Voluntary Agency

14. Domestic violence forum

15. Referral from another refuge

The aim of every agency involved with victims of domestic violence, should be to assist and enable these people to break free from the tyranny they have experienced, catapulting them into complete safety, as a way of life. Anyone can help these vulnerable women especially in this day and age where there are such resources as the internet.

END NOTES

1. https://www.dailymail.co.uk/news/article-3215517/ Brooke-Beaton-face-domestic-violence-campaign- posting-photos-bruises-online.html

2. https://www.avonworldwide.com/supporting-women/ violence-against-women-and-girls

5

Putting Your Life Back Together Again

It is intensely difficult to overcome the horror of being abused. It is therefore an inevitable major challenge to be able to resist the temptation to refuse to become bitter and twisted. Working at the refuge, I saw this manifest in the women I dealt with. If they fell out with one another, they became aggressive and argumentative, as their abusers had been towards them. I remember this one incident in particular. Two of the women who were both residents, physically fought with each other. It stuck in my mind because one of them was holding a baby at the time! I don't know why I did this, but I found myself physically putting myself between them. I suppose it was instinct, because I was concerned for the baby. (Not really the wisest thing I ever did though)! Sometimes, this can also be seen when children are abused. They often grow up to become abusers themselves!

Once you have survived domestic violence, you could very well suffer from so many mixed feelings, that are justifiable, and understandable. This may include feelings of loss as if you are bereaved. Even when a relationship was abusive, in its breakdown it can feel as if there has been a death. In effect there actually has been, as you say goodbye to all the negativity, the restrictive control, and manipulation, as well as the constant need to live while staring death in the face, as a way of life. This normally should feel like a breath of fresh air, and a major cause for celebration. When bad and destructive things are all you are used to however, you may very well grieve the loss of familiar negative circumstances. Surviving the trauma is all about re-training yourself to get used to embracing positive, edifying, uplifting things that build you up rather than tear you down. You will need to get used to a completely new way of thinking and experiencing life.

Characteristically you may have a million mixed feelings.

- You may feel a sense of guilt for the breakup of the relationship, especially if there are children involved. After all you have instigated the split (justifiably so). You will have to learn to let go and release the guilt! It has no place in your new life going forward, and you deserve to shake it off, so you can eventually enjoy your slices of freedom and happiness!

- You may feel confused about the fact that of all the people there are in the world, why this has happened to you. Why did you have to be the one who has gotten caught up in this unhealthy broken type of relationship? Why couldn't you be the one who instead successfully found her Prince charming?

- You may feel angry because you have been unfairly oppressed and treated so badly, by someone close. Suddenly feeling angry feels so right because all that pent-up emotion finds release at long last!

- You may feel as if you are incapable and ill equipped to cope with life. As you were constantly subdued and suppressed you have no idea how to operate apart from this kind of scenario.

- You may feel sad and have much regret because of all

the wasted years, that you cannot get back. It's not as if you can just go back to continuing to be the person you were before you met your abuser.

- You may feel empty inside because apart from the abuse you have suffered, there has been nothing else. How exactly do you fill the void and what do you fill it with?

- You may feel lost because abuse is all you know, and now it has been removed, strangely you have lost a sense of who you are, because you no longer need to be the victim, but you don't remember how to be anything else.

- You feel numb because for so long you had to shut off all your emotions, just to survive the intense pain that had become your way of life.

These different feelings are totally understandable considering all you have been through. Obviously having these feelings for company often for years on end, is bound to have a profound effect on you. After suffering from domestic violence, you will never ever be the same again. You can however learn to be stronger, wiser, better and whole.

SECTION ONE

GETTING LEGAL HELP

When considering the intricate details of all that takes place in a domestically violent relationship, once it breaks down, certain things need to be put in place. This is especially true because as a victim of domestic violence, it is quite likely you are unsure of where you stand, and what your rights are.

To be able to establish the answer to these pressing issues once and for all, it may be a good and helpful idea to get yourself some legal help, and representation. The advantage of this is that it could go a long way to removing the inevitable feeling of helplessness you may feel, replacing it with the unfamiliar feeling of becoming empowered. When you become familiar with what you are entitled to, then inevitably you'll be in a much stronger position, to present and hopefully win your case if you decide it is worth taking things to court. When you are however ignorant regarding these things, then you are so much more likely to settle for and accept much less that you are entitled to!

The other big plus that comes from pursuing things until they have become legitimate, is that it means you will have a record of the things that have happened in your own unique situation. This can all be used as evidence against the abuser if you ever did decide to press charges against him. With the weight of the law now behind you, you have the best chance of seeing justice finally being served, and things working out in your favour.

On the 18th of December 2014 the Government announced that they were bringing out a new law, after having a consultation with the home office. This law has made 'controlling behaviour,' a crime and it is designed to deal with all manner of coercive behaviour that occurs in a domestically violent relationship. This includes controlling victims through social media. Relevant evidence can now be gathered in this way to present to court, and it includes threatening text messages, and bank statements (that prove that financial abuse has taken place). This has become necessary to protect victims from extreme psychological and emotional abuse, which is now being recognised as part of the overall abusive behaviour. When found guilty, the perpetrator can be fined or imprisoned for up to five years.

This has truly become a landmark moment in history. There have been times when domestic violence has not been seen or treated as the hideous crime that it is. At long last it has finally been recognised as a crime to be taken seriously. Now the law covers any pattern of threats, incidents of humiliation and intimidation, including ex-partners using social media to spy on their victims.

This law recognises and highlights the fact, that domestic violence is a violation of the basic human rights of the victim. Domestic violence severely affects and restricts their freedom and desire to be completely independent.

Whether or not the abuser ends up being charged or not is determined by how many times he has offended in this area, and how much he has been guilty of displaying this unacceptable behaviour.

END NOTES

1. Retrieved from https://www.gov.uk/government/news/coercive-or-controlling-behaviour-now-a-crime 29 December 2015 Home Office and The Rt Hon Karen Bradley MP

HOW DOES THE LAW SUPPORT VICTIMS AND PROTECT THEIR RIGHTS?

Every victim of domestic violence is absolutely entitled to live their lives safely, and to be legally protected to ensure that this is the case! Violence directed at you in any way, shape or form, is a crime and should be dealt with as such! Thankfully this is the day and age where very slowly but surely, things are moving in the right direction and becoming more of a reality. Bearing this in mind, there are certain types of legal help available to you, so that you can be free from a life of abuse.

POLICE HELP TO BREAK FREE

When you are in trouble, you do not need to face it alone or deal with it by yourself. You can involve the police by ringing 999, if you are at immediate risk and find yourself in an overwhelming, emergency situation that you cannot cope with. Do not worry about bothering them or hesitate to call if you need someone to help you. Afterall it is their job to protect you.

Women who turned up at the refuge, often did so because they were brought to us by the police who figured it was unsafe for them to remain at the property at that time. Sometimes this was in the middle of the night!

Part of the process of protecting you successfully may entail having to arrest your abuser, and forcibly remove him from the property, especially as he may not go with them willingly! Putting your safety at the forefront will determine how they handle things and proceed. If it so happens that as a result they charge him with a crime, it will most likely be a case of restrictive conditions that are (relevant to your particular situation), will also be attached for good measure!

This makes it much easier to determine if he has violated any of the terms of the conditions he has been set, later on down the line. Once this has been established, he will automatically land himself in more trouble, if he bothers you. The aim of all this is to deter him from continuing to behave abusively towards you, providing an opportunity where perhaps for the first time he can be held to account for his actions against you! Hopefully this development will cause him to think seriously before he chooses to abuse you again. He may feel it is not worth getting himself into trouble with the law, to continue to harass and abuse you. Perhaps wisdom will prevail as he considers the huge implications that such actions will have for him, if he chooses not to behave himself!

END NOTES

1. Women's aid Domestic violence (Your legal rights)
   Revised 2008 p2, p3

TAKING LEGAL ACTION AGAINST YOUR ABUSER

(A brief overview)

Regarding your decision to take legal action against your abuser, unfortunately there are no hard and fast rules about whether the case going to court, will automatically mean you have to attend.   Understandably it may be the last thing on earth you want to do or feel comfortable with. If it is necessary however, looking ahead to your future, going to court may be imperative to adding another layer of defence, against having to remain a victim of domestic violence and deal with this criminal behaviour from the person abusing you! Once you are safe and free, having things put in place legally will mean that if anything goes wrong, the law will be on your side and work in your favour.

It is most likely that you will understandably find the whole court scenario an intimidating ordeal, especially as it will probably be an unfamiliar experience for you. You are however able to choose to take someone with you for moral support. It is worth remembering that although this is a difficult part of your journey on the road to freedom, putting legal things in place will bring you one step closer to being able to get on with the rest of your life, so hang on in there and be encouraged!

Assuming you do have to go to court, you might as well get the most you can out of deciding to go down this route to make your life better! It is worth noting that there are certain legal options that you can choose to take that will help you ensure you keep yourself safe, once you leave the violent relationship.

Sometimes women who stayed with us at the refuge,

or who had moved on to live in their own properties, were granted court orders. These varied depending on which particular aspects of protection were relevant to them and their own unique circumstances at the time, and well as which one would benefit them the most.

Just to illustrate, a lady called Kate was granted a court order that had the main aim of bringing a stop to any violence, threats or intimidation) towards her from her abuser. The order she was given was concerned with ending any rights he had been exercising to date. The order forbade him from being able to have contact with her anymore, as she was now exercising her right to choose to leave the relationship. It covered ending his ability to be allowed to stalk, phone, physically harass, or even come within a certain distance of her! It went even further to also deal with even the possibility of him encouraging other people, including (family and friends) from intimidating her on his behalf because he could no longer do so directly! (Essentially the order was designed to force her abuser to STOP his inappropriate destructive behaviour towards her)! Once she was given this order, successfully getting this bit of legality in place, if he broke the conditions that were attached to it in any way, she could immediately exercise her rights to call the police to assist her, so that they were the ones who dealt with him, so she didn't have to!

Subsequently if he bothered her at all, he could find himself in a sticky position where his options would become, having to pay a fine or go to prison, if he broke which ever relevant conditions were attached to the order she was granted. This would mean that even more weight would be added to any case she decided to bring against him in court.

Susan was another lady who went to court and was granted a different kind of court order, which had a completely different function. She didn't want to move away from the area but preferred to move back into the property, (they had shared as a couple) once she left the refuge. This order was therefore concerned with practically sorting out the domestically violent situation that she found herself in. The order she was granted had the goal of being able to bring categorical clarity to the situation, which she so desperately needed! When it came to the relationship she had been in with her abuser, once it broke down there were inevitable complexities that needed to be dealt with appropriately. One of those complexities included the practicality of sorting out the place that as a couple they had both called home up until now. They could not both obviously continue to live there, so as it had gone to court, there were certain questions that needed to be answered once and for all. Did Susan or her abuser have the right to stay there? Who had to leave? A decision had to be made. This is where out of necessity court intervention became the only answer, to reaching a resolution. Ultimately it was be up to them to have the final say by stating definitively therefore who had the 'legal right,' to stay in the family home, now that the relationship between Susan and her abuser had broken down, due to domestic violence.

Being able to have this order implemented is absolutely, imperative for countless victims to be able to get on with their lives. When things are so bad that they have broken down irrevocably, having one of these is the only way to be able to establish certain vitally important things. Once this order is successfully put in place, then the question of whether you will be able to return to the place you once called home or not, can at last be settled. After-all if you do return, you will want to be able to do so in a safe manner. The last thing you need is having to live with the fear or worry that your abuser will be able to keep turning up and making your life a living hell! No doubt you will want to put the trauma of domestic violence behind you, as you get on with the business of living the rest of your life! The court in granting you a tailor-made specific order so to speak, will provide the necessary means for you to be able to move on and forward, with the legal backing you need to put your mind at rest. Things will hopefully look and feel a lot different when you have the authority of the law to fall back on, if your abuser tries to get up to his old tricks!

- ◆ **FOR FREE LEGAL ADVICE FOR WOMEN CONTACT:**
  Rights of Women (Helping women through the law
  Email: Info@row.org.uk
  Phone: 18001(0207 2516575)

As of the twenty first of January 2019, the UK government is attempting to tackle domestic violence, by bringing in legislation that has been set out in a draft bill. This bill has been published and has the following aims and characteristics:

- To support victims and their families and pursue offenders.
- The new law will include the government definition of domestic violence, specifically including 'economic abuse,' and controlling manipulative abuse.
- A domestic abuse commissioner will be established

to deal with the response to domestic violence issues, including with regard to domestic protection notices and protection orders. These are to further protect victims and restrict offenders and force them to attend rehabilitation, behaviour change programmes and programmes where substance abuse has been a factor.

- It may force offenders to take mandatory lie detector tests on release from prison.

- The law prohibits the cross examination of victims by their abusers in the family court. (Zoe Dronfield campaigned to make courts less traumatic for abuse survivors.) She suffered abuse from her ex who is now in jail. She explained that many women decline going to court because they don't want to be cross examined by their abuser!

- It will provide automatic eligibility for specific measures to support victims as they give evidence in the criminal courts.

- It aims to raise awareness and support victims.

END NOTES

1. https://www.gov.uk/government/news/government-publishes-landmark-domestic-abuse-bill 21 January 2019

2. Women's Aid Federation of England. (Domestic violence Your legal rights) booklet Revised 2008 P3, P10

SECTION TWO

REBUILDING A SOCIAL LIFE

PART ONE

A HEALTHY RELATIONSHIP VERSES AN UNHEALTHY ONE

If you are even considering embarking upon a new relationship after your traumatic ordeal, it is my deepest wish that you will first do some required homework. This entails doing all you can to educate yourself regarding exactly what constitutes a healthy relationship. It is imperative that the painful mistakes of the past are not repeated! It is completely possible to survive the ordeal of domestic violence and come out the other end. The aim and goal though, must be to only ever entertain those relationships that will enrich, bless, and add to your life.

So how on earth do you recognise what a healthy relationship looks like if you haven't exactly had the pleasure of experiencing one? Well perhaps the following can help educate and equip you, enabling you to make better and informed decisions regarding the matter.

HOW DO YOU KNOW WHEN LOVE IS REAL?

- Love is patient.
- Love is kind.
- Love is not jealous, and it does not envy.

- Love does not boast.

- Love is not proud.

- Love is not rude.

- Love is not self-seeking.

- Love is not easily angered.

- Love does not demand its own way.

- Love is not irritable, and it keeps no record of when it has been wronged.

- Love is never glad about injustice but rejoices whenever the truth wins out.

- Love never gives up.

- Love never loses faith and is always hopeful. Love endures through every circumstance.

- Love will last forever. 1 Corinthians 13 (New Living Translation)

HOW TO RECOGNIZE A HEALTHY MAN/WOMAN

- A healthy person exercises self-control so is not therefore obsessed with controlling you instead.

- A healthy person never feels the need to violate your free will and manipulate you at every opportunity.

- A healthy person is respectful of you, (what you want, think and feel).

- A healthy person does not keep moving the goal posts, so when you are with them, you know exactly where you stand.

- A healthy person does not play mind games.

- A healthy person builds you up.

- A healthy person tells you that you are beautiful/handsome.

- A healthy person encourages you to be the best that you can be, in every area of your life.

- A healthy person encourages you to make your own decisions and supports the ones you choose to make.

- A healthy person takes personal responsibility for their own happiness.

- A healthy person is a great support to your life.

- A healthy person understands the art of compromise and practises it often.

- A healthy person is thoughtful towards you.

- A healthy person is usually cheerful and nice to be around.

- A healthy person expresses trust in you.

- A healthy person encourages your interaction with family and friends.

- A healthy person is never afraid to admit when they are wrong. They are not too proud to say the word sorry!

- A healthy person shares household responsibilities including the financial side of things.

- A healthy person respects your right to say no to sex.

- A healthy person is a good parent.

HOW TO RECOGNIZE AN UNHEALTHY MAN/WOMAN

- ◆ An unhealthy person is controlling.

- ◆ An unhealthy person is manipulating.

- ◆ An unhealthy person disrespects you at every opportunity.

- ◆ An unhealthy person plays mind games.

- ◆ An unhealthy person puts you down and makes it their mission to subdue, repress and humiliate you.

- ◆ An unhealthy person makes a habit of shouting at you, even shouting you down if you dare have an opinion or idea of your own.

- ◆ An unhealthy person works at wearing down your self- esteem.

- ◆ An unhealthy person encourages you to be dependent on them.

- ◆ An unhealthy person will not encourage or allow you to make your own decisions.

- ◆ An unhealthy person believes it is your job to make them happy.

- ◆ An unhealthy person calls you degrading names that devalue you, as if you're worth nothing.

- ◆ An unhealthy person never takes personal responsibility for anything.

- ◆ An unhealthy person never does their share, but instead prefers to scrounge off you. They become a drain on your life, much like a leech!

- An unhealthy person throws tantrums, breaks and smashes things, becoming violent when they don't get their own way.

- An unhealthy person is quite happy to use the kids as pawns, as if life is nothing more than a chess game.

- An unhealthy person is often miserable and grumpy, a reflection and measure of what they feel like deep down inside.

- An unhealthy person never trusts you. Mostly this is because they are acutely aware of all that they usually get up to behind your back. Naturally they presume you must be up to the same and worse!

- An unhealthy person works at isolating you, from your family and friends.

- An unhealthy person would rather blame you, than admit they are ever wrong.

- An unhealthy person makes fun of you.

- An unhealthy person is quite happy to steal to get what they want, even if that means being a rapist!

- An unhealthy person is only interested in and responds positively, to their own ideas.

- An unhealthy person believes they are the center of the universe, and therefore it is their right to dominate everything and everyone else.

- An unhealthy person turns the kids against you.

Going into a new relationship after your horrendous ordeal, will inevitably be a big deal and huge step for you. You may have mixed feelings as you overcome the trauma of what you have experienced so far. Once you heal physically, emotionally, and mentally, then you can decide whether you are ready for that next step or not. I encourage you to accept that it is wise to proceed cautiously. There is no need to rush into anything at any point. In-fact the slower you allow any relationship to develop, the more chance you will have to figure things out. Time will afford you the opportunity to dip your toe into the water so to speak. You need to know exactly what you're getting yourself into, before you throw caution to the wind and make any kind of commitment. You should give yourself breathing space to decide if you even want to!

All in all, it will be helpful to you to develop a checklist of questions you need to ask yourself and settle on. This will hopefully set you on the right track and help you to decide, what kind of person you actually want to spend the rest of your life with!

- In life what things matters the most to me?

- Who are the people that are important to me?

- What am I looking for in a relationship and what do I expect from my life's partner?

- What am I no longer prepared to tolerate and put up with?

- How far am I prepared to compromise myself to be in this relationship?

- How far am I prepared to go to maintain this relationship?

- What are the most important qualities that I must find in a life's partner, before I allow myself to get involved?

- Am I happy to stop being me just so I can be what this relationship demands of me?

These are definitely soul-searching questions. As you grow and change as a person, you can always add to this list as you are going along. What you must realize is that as you begin to apply the new skills you have learned during your transformation, you will develop a champagne taste as far as your choices are concerned! This is the crucial point that you need to get to, and definitely the goal you would be wise to keep in mind. As you master this new way of thinking and therefore living, you will inevitably begin to attract good and positive things and people, into your precious life!

It is worth remembering this. There is a vast difference between willingly choosing to submit yourself to someone, fully exercising your free will, versus being oppressed and having your choice snatched away! To summarize, if you feel uneasy about a relationship, there is probably a good reason for that uneasiness. Trust your gut instinct, it could save you a lot of time and heartache.

PART TWO

EMBRACING THE WHOLE
CONCEPT OF RESPECT

Definition of respect: A feeling or understanding that someone or something is important, serious, and should be treated accordingly in an appropriate way. (Merriam Webster. com dictionary).

Coming from a domestically violent background, may have left you completely unfamiliar with the important issue of respect, specifically the lack of it. Learning to understand what it entails is a major weapon in the battle against domestic violence. Once you learn the art of respecting yourself on every level, (physically, emotionally, sexually, mentally) etc.. it will be so much easier to expect and insist on, being respected by whoever you are in a relationship with. A deep, rather than superficial understanding of this truth, is needed and essential. The reason is because you possess the power to set the tone of any new relationships you get involved in, now that you have discovered the treasures of freedom and choice.

Respect means you are now in possession of the ability to make and express your own decisions. You have a right to your own opinions even if that means you do not agree with someone else's! The chances are they won't like it and may therefore get nasty and become aggressive. You however still have the right to communicate what you want to do and say, without the fear of repercussion. You should not be made to feel you will face 'unfavourable consequences,' just because you have chosen to make up your own mind and make a choice! Respect means you can speak about what is on your mind, and even have the audacity to change your mind if you want to!

You are free to make mistakes without someone standing over you in judgement! One of the greatest gifts you could ever have, is knowing unequivocally that you have every right to be yourself completely, without being pressured into anything, or placed in any kind of danger because of the choices you make!

Respect means you are encouraged by the person you are with. You are supported in your relationship to feel good about yourself, and whichever way you choose to live your life. Just because you may choose to share your life, this does not give your partner the license to force you to give up your opinions and choices! This should apply even during those times when you do not agree and share the same views.

When there is no respect it is highly unlikely you will feel safe, secure, happy and as if all is right with the world. It is such a foundational part of what defines a relationship as healthy and loving that its presence or absence, can be the difference between heaven or hell on earth. You should not have to spend any of your time feeling threatened or afraid, whenever your partner is around.

You should be encouraged by your partner to spend time with other people who love and care for you apart from him. This should include family members or friends. It is vitally important to be free to maintain your other relationships, with whoever you decide you want to. Why should you be made to feel as if you must give them up just because you are with him now? You should not feel afraid or controlled by him!

END NOTES

1. Women's Aid Federation of England. (Expect respect) booklet 2008

PART THREE

LEARNING TO STAND UP FOR YOURSELF

Learning to stand up for yourself is about refusing to accept being abused, as your lot in life. It is a skill that is needed if you are going to survive and enjoy your life. It is an art and much needed life skill, to learn how to avoid getting drawn in to relationships that are potentially abusive. There are usually signs early on in the relationship, but if you don't know what you are looking for, these signs can easily be missed.

Learning to stand up for yourself includes the following:

- Doing whatever is necessary to have the freedom to express yourself and admit what you think and feel about different things.

- Being courageous enough to say what you want or do not want in any given situation.

- Making your own decisions about what you want to do in life, and when you want to do it. You should be able to prioritize the things that are important to you, without being told what you can and cannot do especially when it comes to what to eat, wear, who you want to be Etc.

- Being free to say no to being manipulated by people, through emotional blackmail and made to feel bad about exercising your rights. This applies especially if you find yourself agreeing to things that you feel uncomfortable with, and don't really want to do.

-

- When you fail to stand up for yourself, then your very human rights are violated, and you won't even get very simplest things that you are entitled to.

- When you internalize everything including all the frustrations that you feel and don't express yourself, you will find you will have to battle with depression and fear all the time. This has a knock-on effect of negatively, affecting your self-esteem and making you feel bad about you ... most of the time.

HOW DO YOU GET TO THE PLACE WHERE YOU ARE NO LONGER STANDING UP FOR YOURSELF ANYMORE?

It all begins with allowing people to speak to and treat you just any old how, even if that is disrespectfully! The more it happens, the more you get used to it until it becomes your normal habit, unfortunately one not easy to break! Before long, it is almost as if you forget to stand up for yourself, and how to put your needs at least on the same level as the needs of others. It is vital to your well-being, to remember that you matter too, as much as anyone else does.

A relationship will become quite unhealthy when it will only work, when the other person is enabled and allowed to take you for granted, treat you terribly, and get whatever they demand of you! It is not good for them and it is certainly detrimental to your wellbeing.

If you are in a relationship where the other person becomes angry just because you have expressed yourself, then this is a clear indication that it is far from an empowering one! The issue is with them rather than with you. You will however find that as a result, you will have to jump through many more hoops to try to satisfy them. The problem though is that they will keep moving the goal posts, whenever they feel like it. You will never be able to give them whatever they say they want from you. It is a losing battle because you can NEVER win!

When you stand up for yourself it shows that you have respect for yourself. This right here is a major key in your arsenal. When you respect yourself, then others are much more likely to treat you with the respect that you deserve and should expect. Their attitude and behaviour towards you will most likely reflect your own towards yourself!

Obviously if you are not used to standing up for yourself, initially it will be incredibly hard to just start doing so. Once you push past all your fears and doubts however, and bravely make that first move to do so for the first, second and third times, eventually it will become your new habit and way of life. With lots of practice, before you know it, it will become very difficult to fail to continue do so!

One of the best ways to begin the process, is to work out the specific situations and scenarios that you find yourself getting anxious about and intimidated by. This will give you a very helpful indication of what you need to begin to address, to be able to move on with your life. It will essentially give you a starting place. Instead of trying to avoid confrontation at any cost, perhaps you could set yourself realistic goals, regarding what you need to tackle first. The sooner you start, the sooner you will get your life back!

Do yourself a huge favour and learn to relax. Take the time to become an expert when it comes to having to deal with difficult situations. Don't shy away and become a shrinking violet! Instead learn to become more self-confident so that you can stand up for yourself, if ever you find you are being mistreated by anyone. If some one says something degrading to you or humiliates you, don't just accept that and not defend yourself! Dare to refuse to accept their version of things and stand up to them, as you stand up for yourself! This is relevant even if you are a novice, implementing this new strategy, for the very first time.

As we have already established, standing up for yourself will require practicing again and again, especially when it is not something you are used to doing. It is however worth it, when you consider all you stand to gain in the end!

Your heart may beat as fast as a wild fire spreads, but don't allow that to put you off! It may feel like the hardest thing you have ever done in your life but stick with it and carry on anyway. Being able to accomplish this will go a long way to breaking the chains that bind you. The prize that you are reaching for, is the ability to untangle the knots that have kept you tied to the option of being a slave to whatever has stopped you from standing up for yourself!

To begin with, it is a good idea to know what you want to say to the person you need to confront. Go over it in your mind as many times as necessary, till you know the essence of what you want to cover in the conversation. When you start to discuss things, keep it short and to the point, just like your practice session, so that you are not dragged off into a direction you don't want to go in. Look directly at the person you are talking to, no matter how uncomfortable, uneasy and frightened you feel, choose to do it anyway. If you find it easier and necessary, look at their forehead instead of directly into their eyes. They'll never realise where you're actually looking, and it might give you the courage you need, to do what needs to be done. As you practise doing this, even though you may still feel uneasy, it will eventually get easier.

Try to keep the tone of your voice even without any trace of hysterics. Speak directly to them without giving them the impression that you are apologizing for being alive and breathing in the same air as them! Remember you have the right to say your piece, as much as anyone else. Do not backtrack! Rather stick to your guns and follow through with what you start saying, regardless of any pressure you may feel, from having to deal with the situation. It doesn't matter if things don't turn out the way you imagined or hoped. It doesn't matter if they don't fall down before you in utter surrender! It doesn't matter if you don't get the right result! What matters is that you have your say, and stand up for yourself whenever necessary, even in a confrontational scenario! Just remember whose to say they are right, and you are wrong? The fact that you may find them intimidating, does not mean that they are right in what they are saying or doing to you!

Don't let your emotions carry you away and cause you to lose control of yourself or the situation. Don't give in to the whirlwind of over powering emotion that threatens to over-whelm you. Stay dignified and refuse to get cross and upset. Don't be nasty and make them feel you are attacking them. Rather stand your ground and keep saying what you wanted to say. The point is, as you practice more and more and learn from each situation you find yourself in, you will get better at it, and eventually won't even have to think about it. The more you stand up for yourself in the right context, the more positive, healthy, and happy you'll find your life becomes and remains. There is nothing quite like taking back the control you lost, and taking charge of your own destiny, rather than just accepting the destiny someone else says you must have!

When it comes to learning all the various aspects of learning to stand up for yourself, it is important to set yourself new realistic goals, both long and short term. Take the time to consider how you would like your life to improve and end up. Then consider the changes you need to make, to ensure this happens sooner rather than later.

Learn how to express yourself because, holding things inside is unhealthy, and works in the same way that poison does. There is great release and empowerment that comes, from having the opportunity to get things off your chest and out in the open. There is nothing worse than everything hidden and camouflaged, by the cover of darkness! Shedding light on these things will lift an incredible weight off your shoulders, giving you the boost your life needs, and deserves.

Learn also how to face up to the problems that you find yourself challenged by. These include things that have gone wrong, as well as things that you just have to admit, are not working in your life. Doing this will give you the momentum you need, to move forward knowing there certainly can be life after domestic violence!

To conclude this section a helpful exercise to complete would be the one below. It will help you to set some helpful goals that you can work towards.

SITUATIONS WHERE I WOULD LIKE TO START STANDING UP FOR MYSELF MORE

1. ....
2. ....
3. ....
4. ....
5. ....
6. ....
7. ....
8. ....
9. ....
10. ....
11. ....
12. ....
13. ....
14. ....
15. ....
16. ....
17. ....
18. ....
19. ....
20. ....

END NOTES

1. Moodjuice (Being assertive-self help guide) 2009 (Neil Rothwell Forth valley NHS Trust 2005) https://www.moodjuice.scot.nhs.uk/assertiveness.asp

SECTION THREE

LEARNING HOW TO TAKE CARE OF YOURSELF

PART ONE

HOUSING

Once your personal safety is established because you have removed yourself from the domestically violent situation, you are on the path to getting your life back. If you are temporarily in a refuge, this will be your opportunity to consider where you will live once you leave there. The refuge staff can point you in the right direction and assist you, to find housing that is appropriate for your needs.

There are a few options that you could do some research on, to help you decide the issue of your housing. Some of these include moving into a housing association property. All your dealings are then with the relevant housing association. If you have any issues, you contact and deal with them directly.

Alternatively, you could go for a shared ownership, or a low-cost home ownership scheme. This would give you as the tenant, the opportunity to own a share of the property, even while you continue to pay rent at the same time.

Another option would be for you to go for a private rented property from a landlord. Make sure you do your research first though. It is important to ensure the property is owned by a reputable landlord with a good track record. Many of the properties are let through a letting agency or estate agency. They should be able to put you right as they vet the landlords before putting them on their books. Unfortunately going through an agency can however turn out to be expensive. This is especially as you will have to pay rent in advance, as well as leave them a deposit. On top of that the agency of course will charge their fee too! It is not exactly an easy or cheap process!

You will need to decide where you want to be rehoused, or whether you should consider returning to your former property. If you were to return home, it would only be wise to do so, after it has been adapted to cater for you. This could include making physical changes to your home, that would greatly fortify its safety features and maximize its security. It is important to ensure, that if you are to live there, it is nothing but a safe haven, for you and your children.

Some of the things you can do to enhance your safety could include having alarms, panic buttons and a peep hole fitted and put in place at the property. You could have one of the rooms converted into a sanctuary room, (that you could lock yourself in if the need ever arose) if you decided to return home, and things went wrong. To transform a room into a sanctuary, more security could be added by connecting some external grills to the windows and external doors, as well as taking the extra measure of having the locks changed. You may have the hinges of internal doors strengthened, as well as bolts added as well. These changes are options worth looking into, to make sure you give yourself the best chance, to be able to get on with your life in a safe environment.

If you do decide to start again and be rehoused somewhere else, it is wise for you to do your research and familiarize yourself with all the issues that may affect your housing choices.

These will entail the following which you may initially be unfamiliar with:

- Dealing with housing associations or the council. This especially applies to understanding what your rights are and what your responsibilities will be as a tenant.

- You will need to grasp how housing benefit works and the help available to you, as well as become familiar with exactly what you are entitled to. You will need to learn how to stay on top of paying your rent regularly, especially if you have never had to deal with having to do so before. You will also have to pay council tax, but maybe entitled to get help with this.

- You will need to learn how to prevent yourself from becoming homeless, by not understanding the circumstances that could lead to eviction, or having your house repossessed.

You may be able to get help to pay your rent as housing benefit is available to people on a low income. It could help you financially, to remove the burden of having to set up your new home. Any money that you have left can then be used to buy other much needed things. The women I worked with at the refuge were able to buy things like furniture, cookers, fridges, microwaves, iron and board, etc.

- A Budgeting advance loan is one that will be taken back out of any benefits you receive until it is paid back. Phone 0843 5060497

- A Crisis loan must be paid back also and is available for family emergencies. The money will be taken back out of the benefits you receive. Phone: 08000 327952

- For further help regarding housing, contact Shelter. They give practical help and resources regarding housing problems or issues. They can certainly point you in the right direction. www.shelter.org.uk publications 08445152036

- You can also get housing advice from the website below. www.citizensadvice.org.uk/housing Phone 03454040506

FLOATING SUPPORT FROM THE REFUGE

At the refuge where I worked, they provided a service called floating support. This entailed the provision of ongoing support, even when a woman moved into her own property. The team of refuge staff would help her with benefits, getting access to other support agencies, gaining employment, or training and education. This was available for as long as she felt she needed it and was there to offer her moral support.

PART TWO

MONEY MANAGEMENT

As a survivor of domestic violence, you may not have had the opportunity to be able to manage your money properly, if at all. This applies especially if your money was always taken away from you. There are organizations out there who give money advice and can teach you all that you need to know to be able to move forward financially. They can help you with debt issues, as well as give you advice about which benefits would suit your unique circumstances, and how to save money.

The CAP money course is a great example. This course helps you to learn to take control of your money, by learning money management budgeting skills. For further details you can check out the website below. www.capmoney.org

PART THREE

DEVELOP PRACTICAL SKILLS

There are some practical things that need to be done when it comes to learning how to look after yourself. This is especially true when you have been a victim of domestic violence, who has spent time isolated from the rest of the world, and in a bubble. As a survivor, freedom will feel as if a whole new world, (that you didn't even know about) has just become available to you.

Here is a list of practical skills that you need to learn that will help you:

- **KEEP A TRACK OF YOUR SPENDING:**
  You may not have had a lot of experience of dealing with money, as perhaps you were forbidden from handling the financial side of things. To take charge of your finances, you will need to know exactly what is coming in and exactly what is going out. As you embark on this new responsibility adventure, it may be a good idea to keep your receipts, so you can become familiar with how much things cost, and learn to budget accordingly, once you know what you have left over each week and month.

- **LEARN TO SAVE:**
  It will take time to get used to having money to spend, especially if you are used to never having any. As exciting as this may be, try not to get carried away but put some aside for rainy day. You never know when you will have a financial emergency to deal with. It will help if you have a source of money stashed away to take the pressure off! It is always good to save as well so that if you decide you want to spoil yourself sometime, you can plan ahead for that and do so because you deserve it.

- **LEARN TO COOK:**
  Learn to cook some nice, quick and easy recipes, now that you are free to choose what you want to buy, cook and eat. Get yourself some cook books or check out some recipe ideas on the internet. Personally, I love Jamie Oliver's 15 minute meals because they are so

simple to follow. They can be be found on you-tube. There are other cooks on there as well. You can learn so much! So now there is no excuse to not spoil yourself. Spend time having fun experimenting with new ingredients that you haven't tried before, just because you can!

- **LEARN TO MAINTAIN YOUR CAR:**
  If you have a car, learn how to take care of it. Learn how to get it serviced, change the oil, put petrol/diesel into it, all the things that you were probably not allowed to do before. Being able to look after your car will save you money and make things easier in the long run. It will also make you feel more independent and give you a sense of achievement. There are free courses on you-tube, so it doesn't have to be expensive to learn.

- **DECISION MAKING:**
  Learn to consider the pro's and con's (advantages and disadvantages) of things before you make the final decision to do them. This will most definitely take some getting used to, especially if you were never allowed to decide anything in the past. It is worth asking yourself the following questions. Will what you are deciding to do help you in your new life? Can you afford to do it at this particular time? When do you want to do it? How will making this decision improve and add to your life?

- **LEARN TO BE AN INDEPENDENT HANDY PERSON AROUND YOUR NEW HOME:**
  When you move into your new house, buy yourself a tool kit so that you can fix simple things. Get a sewing kit to repair and maintain your clothes. Get yourself a

first aid kit, so that you can take care of yourself if you have a minor accident or feel slightly unwell. Once again there are some free 'handy person' courses on you-tube.

◆ **GET A PHYSICAL CHECK UP:**
Being in an abusive relationship inevitably takes its toll on you, perhaps in ways that you didn't even realize. You want to ensure that you do all you can to recover on every level, physically, emotionally and mentally. Once your health is back on track, you can get yourself into a fitness and a healthy regime. You can learn how to do what is necessary to feel good about yourself, as well as how to become healthy from the inside out, and get the twinkle back in your eye. Inevitably this will affect your self-esteem and self-confidence. When you feel good, you will most likely be at your best and ready to take on and face the rest of your life!

◆ **SEEK ADVICE:** If there are things that you don't know and are not sure about, find someone who knows more about it than you do. Ask questions and get educated so that you can make informed decisions from this point on. You want to be able to make the most of your life from this point on, and there is no reason why you should be content to stay ignorant about anything, ever again! You are free! Learn everything you can about everything!

◆ **LEARN HOW TO DEFEND YOURSELF:**
Coming from a domestically violent relationship has probably left you not knowing how to defend yourself, and therefore feeling vulnerable. Take a self-defense course. This will enable you to protect yourself so

that you know what to do, when you are faced with a threatening situation. This will also help you to grow in confidence, when you are around other people, rather than feeling intimidated and afraid in unfamiliar territory.

- **LEARN HOW TO READ OTHER PEOPLE:**
Practise until you perfect the art of being able to discern the ins and outs of non-verbal communication. Do this until you become familiar with other people's body language. This is especially important when you need to work out if you are in danger or not, so you can take the appropriate action, and remove yourself from any unsafe circumstance.

- **LEARN HOW TO BE RESILIENT:**
Learn how to bounce back from disappointment, setbacks, and hardships as unscathed as possible. Your life is not over after domestic violence although it may feel like it. You need to learn to trade a defeatist attitude, for one that refuses to give up and stay the victim. You can make a success of your life in spite of all that has happened to you. You are a survivor and have come this far! If you continue to be courageous you will never be defeated victim again!

- **LEARN HOW TO RELAX:**
Domestic violence will affect your ability to relax; In-fact it may even eliminate it all together! Take time to develop the skill of total relaxation. This will help you to sleep better. Find effective ways for you to manage stress levels. To be able to do this, you will need to learn to deal with and eliminate crippling anxiety. That means actively seeking to identify anything that makes you feel

anxious. Work out the things that are based on facts, verses those things that are based on assumptions, and will probably never happen in reality! Make a conscious effort to refuse to worry about anything. Be confident that every challenge that comes your way, you will find a way to work it all out! Explore and find things that you enjoy doing and spend time doing them! Relaxation is an important skill that you will have to relearn, especially if you are to live your new life well.

♦ **LEARN HOW TO LIVE YOUR BEST LIFE NOW!**
Set realistic goals for yourself. This will give you direction so that, you can begin your journey to achieving great things with the rest of your life. Don't just wait for some time in the future when you can start enjoying yourself! Instead learn to live each day as if it was your last. Enjoy it to the max and decide that the best days of your life are ahead of you and yet to come! Never ever again allow anyone to tell you otherwise!

♦ **MAKE YOUR EXPERIENCE WORK FOR YOU:**
Your experience although a horrendous ordeal, can be turned into a wealth of wisdom. It will help you to make good and better decisions in the future. Learn how to live your best life now and know that you are an incredible inspiration to others who have felt stuck and hopeless in their situation! Just think of the countless people out there who are desperate to see some light at the end of their particular tunnel. Hearing your story could make the uttermost difference to them. Nothing you have been through should be wasted, as you are now qualified to stand for a prime example of someone who

has been through the mill and successfully come out the other side!

6

A Closing Thought

It is my sincere hope and prayer that after reading this book you are deeply encouraged and have found it to be a helpful resource. It was always my intention to write a book that would serve as a map, for all those who have lost their way because of domestic violence. It is also very important to me, that you realize that there certainly can be life after the horrible trauma you have been through! It is just a question of becoming equipped and having a clear idea about what you want now, as well as working out in what direction you want the rest of your life to go in. Life only gives you so many chances! Being free is a chance worth taking!!! Perhaps you could begin your new journey by attending the freedom programme. This is a very helpful course, designed to educate you especially regarding the whole subject of domestic violence. The idea is that it educates you to better understand what you went through, as well as how to avoid going into a similar situation.

Contact: www.freedomprogramme.co.uk

Phone: 01942 262270

As a victim of domestic violence, you need to understand that what happened, was not your fault! Whatever harm was done, was done to you, your heart and soul, but if you can find a way to make peace with that, then you have won in spite of everything! You are not to blame and you are in no way responsible for what happened to you. Once you have come to terms with things, if you are able, it is helpful to talk about and share your experience. It is a powerful step toward a healthier life that has moved on and forward.

If you have been blessed enough to survive, then there are so many good things ahead of you. It is time to learn new skills and get yourself educated. Don't get stuck in a rut where you don't know or understand things and remain happy with that. Instead gain an in depth understanding that all potential risks of domestic violence towards you, must be minimized and eventually eliminated completely. Your protection and safety are paramount and must become your new priority! Meet new people, build your confidence, self-esteem and self-belief, and make it one of your life's mission to get everything that was taken away from you, restored! If you have children, take a course to brush up on your parenting skills, so that you can spend quality time enjoying the freedom to be with them, without anyone threatening you or them. It is time to build new relationships and a social life that is completely opposite to all you have known, and one that is infused with and underlined by abundant health.

Although no doubt this has been an incredibly harrowing experience, you have the power to decide whether you will allow it to define you or not! You certainly can go from being broken, vulnerable and delicate to healed, restored and strong in time. I encourage you to turn every scar into a bright star that will serve as a beacon to others. This is not the end of you, rather it is a new beginning for you and hopefully for everyone who hears your story! As you get your life back on track, let your new goal become, to make every moment count!

The main aim of this book has been to help domestic violence survivors, find their voice, and ultimately be seen and heard. Consequently, I have decided to include a list which hopefully will encourage you, that this process has at least started. Although so much more needs to be done regarding this issue, there are people that are fighting for change, and this includes some celebrities, who feel very passionately about this subject. They have therefore decided to use their standing, status, and influence, to raise awareness and campaign against the vile thing that is domestic violence against women. Their determination has gone a long way towards bringing it out of obscurity, and into the open. Some of them have a unique understanding of the subject because they have been through it themselves. It reminds me of the saying, "the only way to dispel the darkness, is to run right into it and shine!"

This list therefore includes a brief overview of the involvement of each celebrity.

PATRICK STEWART: (Actor) He grew up in a home that was domestically violent. In fact, he remembers watching his father beating up his mother when he was only five years old. As this happened so often, he became expert at knowing when to move himself to try to shield and protect his mother with his (tiny body), from his father's vicious flying fists. He grew up feeling totally helpless, with an unbelievable burden on his shoulders that no little boy should ever have to carry! This affected him profoundly needless to say!

Now that he is in a better position to do something, he has become a Patron of the charity, Refuge. He works closely with them and has met many survivors of domestic violence, so that he can listen to their particular story. He does all he can to raise awareness regarding the important work of this charity, as well as the threat it is under due to cuts to funding.

OPRAH WINFREY: (Chat show host) She was abused as a child with her ordeal beginning, with a brutal rape when she was the tender age of nine years old. She then suffered from consistent sexual abuse right up to the age of fourteen. Remarkably somehow however she managed to find the strength to overcome such horrendous trauma! She then developed incredible empathy with other vulnerable people as a result. This enabled her to become the chat show host that she is well known for. She has developed her show to such an extent that it now provides all sorts of people with a platform to tell their story no matter how painful. Over the years her guests have included victims of rape, incest, and domestic violence, and she is a great advocate for women to become empowered in their lives.

NICOLE KIDMAN: (Actress) She has become the spokeperson for the UN initiative… "Say no…unite to end violence against women." She has also become the face of their online campaign.

CHARLIZE THERON: (Actress) She grew up in a domestically violent home. Her father who drank, would often come home and threaten her and her mother. As a result, when she was fifteen years old, unfortunately she witnessed her mother shoot her father dead, as this had become the only way to protect them both. As it was totally in self-defence, her mother was not charged for the shooting.

Charlize travelled to the Democratic Republic Of The Congo as a (United Nations Messenger of peace), to raise awareness about domestic violence. She is also a leader of the 'stop rape now,' campaign.

DANIEL CRAIG: (Actor) He has been working hard to raise awareness about domestic violence against women. He works hard on focusing mainly on encouraging men to see things from a women's perspective, and to gain an understanding of where they are coming from. His aim is to instigate a change in men's behaviour as a result.

JAMELIA: (Singer) She was a victim of domestic violence suffering at the hands of a former boyfriend, who beat her up most days. This became her 'norm.' Having her daughter however, gave her the strength and courage to make a change, and leave the relationship for her daughter's sake. She did not want her child growing up in that kind of atmosphere. Jamelia is now a spokesperson for single mothers, campaigning for their rights as she felt she wanted to give something back.

REESE WITHERSPOON: She is the honorary chair of the Avon foundation, which helps to fund domestic violence programmes, that work with women, suffering from abuse. She is also an Avon global ambassador. Taking on her role she urged the government of the United Kiingdom to do more to prevent violence against women. She also launched 'The empowered bracelet,' to raise funds for the work of the Avon foundation. She helped launch the 'refuge campaign,' four ways to speak out against domestic violence. Her involvement has raised the awareness about domestic violence to a level it probably would not have received without her input and support.

TERRY CREWS: (ACTOR) He is a survivor of sexual assault and grew up as a victim of domestic violence. As a child he watched his father punch his mother in the face. Now as an adult, he uses his platform to address the issue of 'toxic masculinity,' and the role that men play in ending violence against women. His willingness to be vulnerable in total honesty, as he shares his testimony has given him maximum impact in his endeavours.

ANNIE LENNOX: She has been involved in the fight against domestic violence by urging the United Kingdom government, to work and pledge an end to global violence against Women.

PETER GABRIEL: He supports the campaign 'stop violence against women. This also includes the campaign, 'to resolve the disappearances and murders of thousands of women, who would otherwise be forgotten!

ANGELINA JOLIE: She works as special envoy for the UN, and within the role she has met many victims of sexual violence and worked to raise awareness of the issue.

DAVID SCHWIMMER: He feels very strongly about men taking their responsibility, regarding violence against women. He also sits on the board of the rape foundation which works towards treatment, prevention and education.

VANESSA EAGLE: She is well known for doing a film documentary called 'love you to death.' It tells the unbelievable stories of 87 women in Britain who died at the hands of their male partners. As a skilled film maker, she focused on highlighting the stories of women who are gone but must never be forgotten. This keeps the issue of domestic violence in the limelight.

END NOTES

1. Retrieved from

https://www.hellomagazine.com/celebrities/2019020867704/patrick-stewart-opens-up-domestic-abuse/ n.d

2. Retrieved from

https://www.learningliftoff.com/overcoming-obstacles-what-oprah-winfrey-learned-from-her-abusive-childhood/

3. Retrieved from

http://www.unwomen.org/en/partnerships/goodwill-ambassadors/nicole-kidman

4. Retrieved from

https://unchronicle.un.org/authors/charlize-theron

5. Retrieved from

http://www.mtv.co.uk/srs/news/these-awesome-celebs-arent-afraid-to-speak-up-about-violence-against-women
November 24th 2015

6. Retrieved from

https://www.dailymail.co.uk/tvshowbiz/article-2760028/Jamelia-admits-scars-domestic-abuse-forever.html
by Emily Sheridan 17th of Sep 2014

7. Retrieved from

https://www.telegraph.co.uk/news/celebritynews/6709714/Reese-Witherspoon-visits-Parliament-to-campaign-on-domestic-violence.html 02 Dec 2009

8. Retrieved from

https://www.peaceoverviolence.org/updates-impact/terry-crews
27th of September 2018

9. Retrieved from

https://16days.thepixelproject.net/16-celebrities-supporting-and-fighting-for-the-cause-to-end-violence-against-women/By Regina December 10th of 2011

10. https://www.vanessaengle.com/love-you-to-death BBC 2015

BIBLIOGRAPHY

1.https://www.christianpost.com/news/god-saved-me-woman-forgives-ex-boyfriend-who-stabbed-her-32-times.html by Morgan Lee 24th of October 2013

2.https://www.independent.co.uk/news/uk/politics/michelle-thompson-rape-age-14-account-story-video-speaker-john-bercow-cry-tears-a7463786.html by Jon Stone 8th of December 2016

3.https://www.theguardian.com/uk-news/2015/aug/17/man-in-court-alleged-stabbing-acid-attack-ex-girlfriend Monday 17th of August 2015

4.https://www.dailymail.co.uk/news/article-3364457/Thug-stamped-pregnant-girlfriend-killing-baby-refused-abortion-GUILTY-accomplice-savage-attack.html By Amanda Williams 17th of December 2015

5.https://www.mirror.co.uk/news/uk-news/pensioner-horrifically-scarred-after-wife-5324460 By Ben Kendall 13th of March 2015

6. https://www.sofeminine.co.uk/key-debates/silence-hides-violence-campaign-against-domestic-abuse-s1555443.html By Maria Bell 8th of September 2015

7.https://people.com/music/tina-turner-ike-abusive-relationship-risked-life/ By Jorden Runtagh October 26th 2017

8.https://metro.co.uk/2017/02/17/viewers-praise-boy-george-for-brave-comments-about-domestic-abuse-in-his-family-6456190/ By Troy Nankervis 17th of Feb 2017

9.https://www.bbc.co.uk/news/uk-england-lincolnshire-46387407 29th of November 2018

10.https://www.cps.gov.uk/london-north/news/mother-first-be-convicted-female-genital-mutilation 1st of Feb 2019

11.https://www.nhs.uk/conditions/female-genital-mutilation-fgm/ n.d

12.https://thetab.com/uk/2018/02/07/the-case-of-molly-mclaren-stabbed-75-times-by-her-ex-for-breaking-up-with-him-60303 n.d

13. (Macmillan Dictionary) 2009 Springernature Ltd

14.What is a forced marriage? The forced marriage unit www.fco.gov.uk/forcedmarriage n.d

15. Claire Throssell on the Victoria Derbyshire show.

https://www.youtube.com/watch?v=HjLjn4Iy4MU

16.https://www.instylemag.com.au/charlize-theron-family-mother-killed-her-father By Tina Burke n.d

17.https://www.theguardian.com/society/2018/apr/10/ellie-butler-unlawfully-killed-inquest-ben-butler By Diane Taylor 10th of April 2018

18.https://www.mirror.co.uk/news/uk-news/sian-blake-arthur-simpson-kent-8974411 By Ben Rossington and Gemma Mullin 4th of October 2016

19. https://www.news.com.au/lifestyle/real-life/true-stories/mumoftwo-dies-two-years-after-her-soulless-boyfriend-set-her-on-fire/news-story/8890ab91be35855ce73282ac77963faf June 29th 2017

20.https://news.sky.com/story/man-jailed-for-life-over-double-murder-outside-matalan-store-in-cardiff-10784992 Tuesday 28th of Febuary

21.https://www.hellomagazine.com/celebrities/2019020867704/patrick-stewart-opens-up-domestic-abuse/ Last modified on 2019-02-08

22.https://www.independent.co.uk/news/world/africa/oscar-pistorius-trial-athlete-scared-girlfriend-reeva-steenkamp-9212563.html n.d

23.https://www.learningliftoff.com/overcoming-obstacles-what-oprah-winfrey-learned-from-her-abusive-childhood/ Jan 7, 2015

24.http://www.mtv.co.uk/srs/news/these-awesome-celebs-arent-afraid-to-speak-up-about-violence-against-women November 24th 2015

25.https://www.dailymail.co.uk/tvshowbiz/article-2760028/Jamelia-admits-scars-domestic-abuse-forever.html by Emily Sheridan 17th of Sep 2014

26.https://www.telegraph.co.uk/news/celebritynews/6709714/Reese-Witherspoon-visits-Parliament-to-campaign-on-domestic-violence.html 02 Dec 2009

27.https://16days.thepixelproject.net/16-celebrities-supporting-and-fighting-for-the-cause-to-end-violence-against-women/ By Regina 10th of December 2011

28. https://www.vanessaengle.com/love-you-to-death BBC 2015

29. Supporting victims (Walsall Domestic Violence Forum) which unfortunately closed down on May the 4th 2016.

30. Pat Craven (Living with the Dominator) 2008 Freedom publishing

31. Victim Support (Domestic violence leaflet) 2018

32. Women's Aid Federation (The Survivor's Handbook) The print version revised in June 2009

33. Women's Aid Federation of England. (Domestic violence Your legal rights) booklet Revised 2008 P3, P10

34. Women's Aid Federation of England. (Domestic violence The risks to children booklet Revised 2008

35. Women's Aid Federation of England. (Expect respect) booklet 2008

36. (Corner house counselling service) Play therapy Information leaflet n.d

37. (Victim support) Vev leaflet n.d

38. Walsall safeguarding children's board (What is trafficking) leaflet n.d

39. Moodjuice (Being assertive-self help guide) 2009

(Neil Rothwell Forth valley NHS Trust 2005) Retrieved from

https://www.moodjuice.scot.nhs.uk/assertiveness.asp

40. (New Living Translation) 1996

41. (Merriam Webster.com dictionary) 1978

42. Changing pathways: https://www.changingpathways.org/refuge 2016

43. Birmingham and Solihull women's aid: https://bswaid.org/ n.d

44. Black country women's aid: https://www.blackcountrywomensaid.co.uk 2019

45. Bristol women's aid:

https://www.womensaid.org.uk 2015

46. Cheshire without abuse:

https://www.cheshirewithoutabuse.org.uk/contact 2018

47. Coventry haven women's aid:

https://www.Coventryhaven.co.uk n.d

48. Derbywomen's centre: https://www.derbywomenscentre.co.uk n.d

49. Glasgowwomensaid: https://www.glasgowwomensaid.org.uk 2009

50. Hestia: https://www.hestia.org/brightsky n.d

51. Harbour middlesborough: https://www.myharbour.org.uk/ 2019

52. Kent oasis women's refuge: https://www.oasisdaservice.org n.d

53. Leeds women's aid: https://www.leedswomensaid.org.uk n.d

54. Manchester womensaid: https://www.manchesterwomensaid.org.uk 2017

55. National womensaid: https://www.womensaid.org.uk/ 2015

56 Nottinghamshire womensaid: https://www.nottswa.org 2015

57 North Kirklees womens refuge: https://connecthousing.org.uk 2019

58. Nuneaton & Bedworth womensaid: https://www.refuge.org.uk/ 2017

59. Panahghar Asian Womens refuge: https www.safehouse.org.uk 2008

60. Roshni Refuge for Asian women https://www.roshnibirmingham.org.uk n.d

61. Sandwell womensaid 2019

62. Solace womensaid: https://www.solacewomensaid.org n.d

63. Staffordshire womens aid: https://www.staffordshirewomensaid.org/ 2019

64. The Haven Wolverhampton: https://www.havenrefuge.org.uk n.d

65 The Pathway Project: Talktoeve.pathway@virgin.net n.d

66. Cap Money course: https//www.capmoneycourse.org n.d

67. Child first: https//www.childfirst.org n.d

68. Childhood domestic violence association: https//www.cdv.org n.d

69. Childline: https://www.childline.org.uk n.d

70. Claiming maintenance safely: https://www.gingerbread.org.uk 2017

71. Priory group: https://www.priorygroup.com 2019

72. Nspcc: https://www.nspcc.org.uk 2019

73. https://www.karmanirvana.org.uk 2018

74. Gingerbread: https://www.gingerbread.org.uk 2017

75. Modern slavery: www.modernslavery.org 2018

76. Ikwro: http://ikwro.org.uk 2019

77.National centre for domestic violence: www.ncdv.org.uk 2018

78. National Express: https://nationalexpress.com 2019

79. National rail: https://www.nationalrail.co.uk n.d

80. https://www.stalkinghelpline.org 2016

81. No panic: https://www.nopanic.org.uk 2018

82. Play therapy uk: https://playtherapy.org.uk 2017

83. Police: https://www.west-midlands.police.uk n.d

84. Rape crisis: https://rapecrisis.org.uk 2019

85. Relate: https://www.relate.org.uk n.d

86. Respect: https://www.respect.uk.net 2016

87. Rights of women: https://www.rightsofwomen.org.uk 2017

88. Tax credit office: https://www.inlandrevenue.gov.uk n.d

89. The freedom programme: www.freedomprogramme. co.uk 2018

90. The hideout: https.www.thehideout.org.uk n.d

91. The samaritans: https://www.samaritans.org n.d

92. the snowdropproject: https.www.snowdropprojectt.co.uk 2017

93. Trident: https://www.reachthecharity.org.uk 2017-2019

94. victim support: https://www.victimsupport.org.uk n.d

95. Women's aid: https://www.womensaid.org.uk 2015

96. Visual evidence for victims: http://www.theglade.org.uk/ visual-evidence-for-victims/ 2019

97. Avon the company for women: https://www. avonworldwide.com/supporting-women/violence-against-women-and-girls 2019

ABOUT THE AUTHOR

Diane Wilkie is a freelance writer and author. She wrote *The Only Arranged Marriage*, the authorized biography of Raj Jarrett, Co-authored *Run For Your Life*, an exciting African mystery novel, full of intrigue and suspense, and trouble in paradise. She also wrote *Knocking On Heaven's Door*. She writes for several other publications that inspire about marriage, raising twins, as well as wisdom and life tips. She lives in Birmingham England with her husband and twin sons. For further details and to get help to write your life story or that of someone else, you can contact her by visiting her website at: www.writeservice4u.wordpress.com

TO CONTACT THE AUTHOR

Email: dee.wilkie7@hotmail.co.uk

Visit: survivedomesticviolence.simplesite.com

If you find yourself in an emergency situation, do not hesitate to call the police on 999.

If the book surviving domestic violence has helped you in any way, please do get in touch as I would love to hear from you.

OTHER BOOKS BY THE AUTHOR

Run for your life! By Gloria Ekwulugo and Diane Wilkie. This is the unforgettable story of the ongoing tug of war between good and evil, and Obi's journey from brokenness to destiny. Obi's introduction to life is plagued by poverty and suffering, in the heart of Africa. He therefore becomes obsessed with making it big in life. He naively gets involved in one of the quickest ways to apparently make money and climb to the top. He is introduced to a completely unfamiliar world where he progresses at rocket speed. In an instant his life changes direction, and he is thrust into the terrifying reality that he is in way over his head but it is too late to turn back! He begins to receive visits from mighty invisible spirit beings that torment and abuse him. Desperate, battered, and just about to walk through death's door, he comes face to face with the most powerful person he has ever met. Is it a too late for Obi?

To order your copy please visit: www.runforyrlife.wordpress.com

Knocking On Heaven's Door *by Diane Wilkie*
ISBN: 978-0-9930876-6-0

Knocking On Heaven's Door invites everyone to learn the art of praying simply, effectively and to actually enjoy the experience. Often prayer is perceived as complicated and therefore only to be embraced by experts! However true heartfelt prayer should be simplicity itself and of great interest to beginners also. This is an indispensable guide detailing what prayer is, how it works, and the different types of prayer methods and strategies, that can be explored even by a novice. Whether you are simply curious about prayer, or seriously considering adopting it as a way of life, it is a handy manual that will equip you to achieve personal victory in all areas of your life. It will challenge, bless, and encourage you to pray more and better, making a difference and having a positive effect on our world!

You Learn How To:
- Achieve prayer success using specific strategies
- Become familiar with the full armour of God
- Fight effectively and gain victory in spiritual warfare
- Understand conditions for answered prayer
- Receive revelation and guidance from an unlimited God

To order your copy please visit:
www.nockingonheavensdoor.word.com

Trouble In Paradise *by Gloria Ekwulugo and Diane Wilkie*
ISBN: 978-0-9930876-0-8

This roller coaster ride of romance, adventure and tragedy fill

this gripping story from beginning to end. Commencing in the paradise of Jamaica it concludes in the United Kingdom the apparent land of promise. Cloretta born to a rich family, knows nothing about going without! Leroy, poor and from the wrong social class has nothing to offer her. They fall in love and develop an unrelenting determination to be together against all odds! However their fiery, volatile relationship threatens to be a force capable of destroying them both! Cloretta inevitably becomes a candle that is dangerously close to being extinguished by the wind that is Leroy. Never did she dream that the price for love might prove to be so high. Passion sweeps her off her feet, and inevitably into a life-changing drama of epic proportions! Cloretta must choose between living her dream or escaping the nightmare.

To order your copy please visit:
www.troublenparadisewordpress.com

ALSO BY OPEN SCROLL PUBLICATIONS

It's Your Time (Your Generation Awaits You)
by Michael Ekwulugo
ISBN: 978-0-9930876-0-8

They say that there's one born every minute. And according to the Bible, each one born, is born a winner. Before your debut on earth, your success had already been settled in heaven. But surviving to succeed at things you were never called to do in this life, is to fail before you've even begun! You've got one life. One opportunity to partner with God and make something spectacular out of your life. There is simply no time to waste. After reading this book, the next voice the world hears... will be yours!

In this humorous and insightful volume, learn how to:
- Discover, develop and deploy your hidden gifts
- Eliminate the 7 greatest threats to your destiny
- Break free from self-destructive thoughts, patterns and habits
- Manage daunting but essential transitions in your life
- Prepare and position yourself for life-changing opportunities

For more information and to order your copy please visit:
www.ekwministries.co.uk or amazon.co.uk

*D*ear reader/writer,

I would like to take this opportunity to thank you for supporting one of our newest authors.

Here at Open Scroll Publications, we specialise in assisting talented writers to fulfil their dreams and aspirations. The creative process is hard enough as it is without having to worry about getting your masterpiece published once you're finally done. That's why Open Scroll Publications was formed. We demystify the process of getting published, and give a literary voice to those who would otherwise be muted in obscurity.

Our list of gifted writers is rapidly growing, and I would like to invite you to consider becoming our next distinguished author. So, whether you're working on a novel, a children's book, a poetry anthology, or an inspirational non-fiction piece, why not take a leap of faith and contact us? We would love to hear from you.

For more information, please visit us at:
www.openscroll.co.uk
info@openscroll.co.uk
Phone: 01213502422
        07506677504

Or write to us at:
Open Scroll Publications Ltd,
Kemp House,
160 City Road,
London, EC1V 2NX.